THE CENTRAL SCHOOL OF
SPEECH AND DRAMA

UNIVERSITY OF LONDON

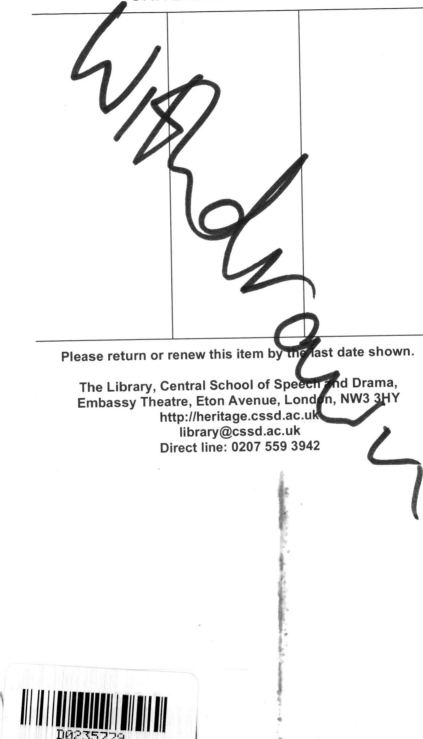

The Decorative Tradition

The Decorative Tradition

Julian Barnard

The Architectural Press
London

For my parents

by the same author
Victorian Ceramic Tiles
(*Studio Vista*)

ISBN 0 85139 134 6
© Julian Barnard 1973
First published 1973
Filmset and printed in Great Britain
by BAS Printers Limited, Wallop, Hampshire

Contents

Acknowledgements

My thanks are due to the many people who gave permission for the photographs to be taken for this book, particularly plates 17, 18, 19, 20, 70, 98, 99 and 106, which are from books in the Victoria & Albert Museum, London. I am also grateful to them for permission to reproduce plates 5 and 57 from their collection. I am also grateful to the following for permission to reproduce photographs: Architectural Press plates 12, 13, 53, 54, 100, 132, 133 (photos H. de Burgh Galwey); 6, 11, 34 (photos Sam Lambert); 129 (photo Dan Cruickshank); Distillers Company plate 2; Henry Grant plate 134 (architect F. Millett); Robert McKinstry & Associates plate 89 (photo R. J. Anderson); Pilkington Bros. plate 135.

It will be noted that a majority of the buildings illustrated are from the London area—there are very few provincial variations in this kind of architecture and those selected for this book are typical examples. If there are some glaring omissions it is not deliberate! No doubt the reader will find local examples readily enough.

I would like to thank all those who directly or indirectly have helped with this book. In particular, Colin Amery, Miss Constable, John Dawson, Sue Dawson, Dr Mark Girouard, Godfrey Golzen and the Lathams.

1 Function versus Decoration

At the present time we are at great pains to preserve the old architecture in our cities, just when it is falling into disrepair and becoming obsolete. Functionally it may have reached the end of its useful life, but there are other things about it that are attractive to us now. In the case of Victorian architecture, with which this book is concerned, what we cherish is the exuberance and visual delight of decoration—the very element that has been rejected in the architecture of the last fifty years. This rejection has been so profound that though we increasingly seek to preserve Victorian buildings we do not like to admit why we do so. Such an admission would call into question what are seen as the fundamental virtues of modern architectural theory, the rationality, economy and simplicity of form that characterise contemporary architecture: all the dogma which is associated with the Modern Movement.

For more than half a century we have been committed to modern architecture with its clean, uncluttered lines, stripped of ornament and the regular forms derived naturally and economically from the technological possibilities of mass production. But the obstinate fact remains that the public have never liked this kind of architecture and consciously or otherwise they regard the bleak, anonymous environment it so often produces with a hostility that expresses itself in vandalism and neglect. Given this situation and the fact that architects have by no means been unaware of it, why have we been saddled with it for so long? One must look here towards the influence the theoreticians exerted on a whole generation of architects before and after the war. By being highly selective in the choice of material the protagonists of modern architecture were able to promote the view that their thinking was both essential and inevitable. A line of development existed which could be traced through the nineteenth century and which led directly to those revered masters Gropius, Le Corbusier and Mies van der Rohe. Architecture that did not fit the theory was dismissed or ignored.

The basis of this argument was the supposition that just before the time of the First World War a cultural revolution took place from which we have never looked back; the odd glance over the shoulder, perhaps, but no more. In essence this revolution was the final commitment to the industrial technology of the machine age. This led to the redefinition of architectural theory, the rejection of superficial

1. Typically decorative building in brick and terracotta, Bristol Centre

2. Whisky distillery, Isle of Islay, Scotland, basically a functional structure; *Distillers Co. Ltd*

ornament and the assumption of aesthetic principles based on functionalism and pure form: the well documented story of the evolution of the International Style. One of the prophets of the new age was Adolf Loos, whose essay *Ornament and Crime*, published in 1908, was a banner for the storm troops. 'I have therefore evolved', wrote Loos, 'the following maxim and pronounce it to the world: the evolution of culture marches with the elimination of ornament from useful objects'.* Loos analysed ornament and decoration† as an expression of degenerate emotion; to him it represented a primitive urge (like body painting or graffiti), which had to be outgrown and rejected as civilisation came of age. Among other things he made an important distinction between the Greeks, whom he abused for their attention to decorative detailing, and the Romans, who were lauded for their feats of structural engineering and the inventiveness they applied to the plan.

Another factor in the creation of modern architectural theory was the assumption that if a building was designed on purely functional lines the form would follow of its own accord. And since the structure evolved logically it would carry with it a new kind of beauty. From these ideas developed such catch-phrases as 'form follows function' and 'a functional aesthetic'. The beauty of modern architecture was to be found in the simplicity and economy of design: the beauty that the Futurists had seen in cars and locomotives, the beauty of man's rational mind imposing itself upon the chaos of nature. But above all else it was decoration that was under attack. For Loos, ornament was the symbol of a corrupt mind which perverted the purity of reason and destroyed the logic of machine-age architecture. This idea gained universal acceptance and was of primary importance in the growth of the Modern Movement.

To show that modern architecture, with its rejection of ornament and decoration, had a proper ancestry, historians have paid a lot of attention to the work of the Victorian pioneers whose buildings foreshadowed many of the elements that are characteristic of twentieth-century thinking in design. Men like Telford, Brunel and Paxton and the engineers responsible for Victorian warehouses, bridges and iron-frame buildings have been seen as the precursors of the modern school of architects. These engineers used materials such as iron and glass to a new performance standard and ignoring the contemporary problems of style created an architecture based on reason and structural logic. But to concentrate on this aspect of Victorian building—what has been called the *Functional Tradition***—means that another stream of thought has been overlooked. For the purposes of contrast this may be thought of as the *Decorative Tradition*.

This title, the Decorative Tradition is necessarily imprecise. It is rather false to speak of two separate traditions in the nineteenth century when the opposition between functional and decorative

* Quoted from Reyner Banham: *Theory and Design in the First Machine Age*, Architectural Press; 1960.
† In the context of this book, these two words, ornament and decoration are used synonymously.
** J. M. Richards, *The Functional Tradition*, Architectural Press; 1958.

architecture is only really apparent in the context of subsequent theory. In the nineteenth century there was a recognised hierarchy with utilitarian, unornamented and basically functional buildings (such as warehouses and mills) at the bottom of the ladder and buildings with increasingly elaborate decorative styles in the various positions on the rungs above. It is hardly reasonable to treat with one sort of building except in the context of the rest. And yet, since most of the architecture of the twentieth century has consciously aligned itself with the 'functionalism' of the most basic kind of Victorian architecture it is convenient to examine the decorative aspects of architecture as a separate tradition.

Properly speaking, as J. M. Richards showed in his book of that title, the Functional Tradition was concerned with buildings that did not seek to elaborate their basic form in any way. Whether a simple arch of a viaduct or the stark façade of a warehouse with regularly placed windows, the structure and the material became the totality of the aesthetic expression. Simple forms were simply beautiful. The purity of this kind of construction was taken up by the architects of the Modern Movement. The form of the building became coincident with the structural system employed and was expressive of the internal spaces, their use and disposition. As Robert Venturi says, in the Modern Movement 'form was merely the result of a logical process by which the operational needs and the operational techniques were brought together'.* In the event this was a rather dry combination of functional requirements and building technology that left little room for imagination and visual interest. Architecture assumed the status of a science.

The Modern Movement abandoned the tradition whereby painting, sculpture and what William Morris called 'the lesser arts of life' were combined in architecture, the 'mother of the arts'.† The pseudo-scientific theories of twentieth century architecture emerged partly as a reaction against the emotional indulgence and overdecoration of the Victorians but even more as the child of the honeymoon between the artist and the concepts of the machine age. The products of the machine age were felt to be more honest, more true to the nature of the material and displaying greater creative integrity than the kind of decoration employed by the Victorians. The advocates of modernism worked on the premise that superficial ornamentation complicated mechanical production and therefore had to be eliminated. When we speak of modern architecture being revolutionised by factory production, what we mean is the regulation of the design specification (materials, dimensions etc.) to fit the requirements of the machine. One cannot help thinking of tails wagging dogs, but the consequence is that the architect today finds himself primarily concerned with a system of design that will use standardised units to their best advantage. Thus grid layouts are devised with reference to trolleys made by a certain company, the standard sizes of glass for

* Venturi, Robert. *Learning from Las Vegas*, MIT 1972.
† The idea that true architecture was closely related to all forms of artistic endeavour was central to the thinking of the nineteenth century and was advocated most strongly by Ruskin, see p. 44.

curtain walling or the repetition of prefabricated units. These sort of factors are a considerable constriction on the creative freedom of the architect and in so many of these glass-walled-high-rise-office-blocks he ends up applying a great part of his ingenuity to finding novel methods for suspending the unfortunate window cleaners. The architect has little more to do than juggle the bits until they go together, selecting the details from a package deal of mechanical requirements. The outcome of this idea of functional architecture is to treat people as machines, hence the concentration on anthroprometrics and space standards. The result is a complete denial of the individual. The remaining virtue of Victorian decorative architecture is that it encouraged individuality.

The architects of the Functional Tradition thought primarily in terms of space. A building was designed to provide an enclosed shelter with space allocated to different activities. But this is only one elementary aspect of architecture, at least as far as the Victorians were concerned. What distinguishes the Functional Tradition from the Decorative Tradition is that in the latter case a far greater emphasis was placed upon the visual quality of the structure. As Ruskin said, 'all architecture proposes an effect upon the human mind, not merely a service to the human frame'.* Thus, to the Victorians, real architecture, by definition, was not only serviceable but something both ornamental and beautiful. The strictly functional structures of the Industrial Revolution, the warehouses, mills, bridges and viaducts, were not seen as belonging to an alternative stream of architectural thinking, they were simply not really regarded as architecture at all. The engineers who designed such structures were highly skilled men who provided a necessary service in an industrial society but their work had little to do with the *art* of architecture. Were Ruskin to see the buildings of the twentieth century he would, no doubt, quite simply conclude that architecture was dead.

The building designed for the 1862 Exhibition (on the site of the Victoria and Albert Museum) provides an instance of the animosity that was engendered when the engineer tried to usurp the position of the architect. The Royal Commissioners (headed by Henry Cole) gave Captain Fowke, a military engineer, the task of designing the structure. No doubt the appointment offended the architectural profession and some of the criticisms were simply the result of injured pride. 'The house the Fowke built' was called a burlesque upon architecture; the most worthless and vilest parody of architecture that was ever produced—'there is not a railway-engine house in existence that would not scorn to be compared with it'—the paltry degeneracy of the Fowke structure showed a 'poverty of conception and a palpable ignorance of all architecture'—something surely needed to be done to 'architecturalise all this dreary commonplace', to 'transform this genuine ugliness into beauty'.†

This was not an attack on all engineers. As the *Art Journal* conceded: 'Captain Fowke may be a first-rate engineer and his presence just

* Ruskin, John. *The Seven Lamps of Architecture*, Complete Works Vol. VIII, 1903; p. 27.
† Remarks from the *Art Journal*, New Series, Vol I, 1862; pp. 46–7.

now might be of inestimable importance somewhere in the neighbourhood of the northern bank of the St Lawrence'. But his incursion into the province of the architect was not to be tolerated. Engineering was a useful *science*, certainly, but it was not to be compared with the *art* of architecture. On occasion this put the architect in rather a false position; Digby Wyatt, for instance, wondered whether he could make any real contribution to Brunel's work at Paddington station (1852–4) and ended up designing decorative motifs for the metalwork.

The separation is even more pronounced in the case of St Pancras (1865–71) where Gilbert Scott's hotel refuses any kind of compromise with the station that it hides. W. H. Barlow's record-breaking span of 240 ft was designed with the simplicity of the best modern engineering style, satisfying well enough the functional requirements. But the hotel, seeking that subtle combination of beauty and utility, reverts to historicism and the elaborate details of the Gothic Revival. Today, neither building needs praise or condemnation, the exciting thing is the contrast between the styles and the ideologies that produced them. Scott, the most prolific of the Gothic 'speculators', also designed the Albert Memorial. (3, 4: numbers refer to illustrations). The memorial, the station and the hotel cover the range of beauty, utility and their combined forces acting in concert to produce what the Victorians regarded as real architecture.

Thus, in a sense, the Decorative Tradition stands for what architecture was always known to be before the revolution of the Modern Movement. The apparent antithesis between function and decoration would have had no meaning for the Victorians since, inasmuch as they would have understood the idea at all, they regarded aesthetic pleasure* as an essential ingredient of the function in all true architecture. A typically Victorian approach to decoration is here expressed by William Emerson:

3. Albert Memorial, London, by Sir Gilbert Scott, 1872

Sculpture is the very soul and life of architecture; without it ancient buildings would not speak to us in the eloquent way they do. The separation of the soul from the body means death; and architecture divorced from sculpture is deprived of the light of the sun of intellectuality, and cannot rise to the ideal or suggest a higher life, it is debased and dead.†

Again it is stressed that architecture without decoration is not architecture at all. It was because this opinion was held so universally that almost all the buildings of the second half of the nineteenth century attempted to claim some kind of decorative style, to employ some form of ornament. It has already been suggested that there was a definite hierarchy in architecture and it is easy to see that decorative forms that were used for prestige buildings were quickly imitated in the lower categories of architecture and a borrowed grandeur filtered through to the meanest designs. When Ruskin pontificates

* John Gloag in his book *Victorian Taste* (A & C Black, 1962), suggests that comfort was a ruling force behind Victorian thinking. 'Style', he says, 'satisfied the Victorian love of display, gratifying the eye by a parade of richness and technical skill and becoming a visual ingredient of comfort.' (p. 123). It is part of the puritanism of modern architecture that we find no such comfort in twentieth-century buildings.

† Emerson, W. *National Association for the Advancement of Art and its Application to Industry*, 1888; p. 139.

4. Detail: a decorative extravaganza with no functional purpose

and lays down the law as to what architecture should be he is speaking only of the acme of architectural achievement—the law courts, churches and government offices. But the architects who designed such buildings called the tune for the rest of the profession and influenced the thinking of all those who were concerned in the design of buildings. This necessarily causes some confusion; when Victorian critics speak about architecture they generally refer to the grandest structures, but it is important to examine the totality of the situation and to see the theoretical background to the whole body of Victorian architecture. The essential unifying factor was the use of decoration and the emphasis that was placed upon the visual impact of a design. It is this general condition of architectural theory that has been termed the Decorative Tradition.

In nineteenth-century architecture, ornament and decoration were used to explore the association between objects and their symbolic meaning. By the use of sculpture, painting and other forms of decoration architecture was able to express particular ideas and values. Modern architecture, by reaction, has chiefly pursued form and formalism for its own sake—whatever the aesthetic theory it is generally devoid of any literal meaning; the visual form cannot be trans-

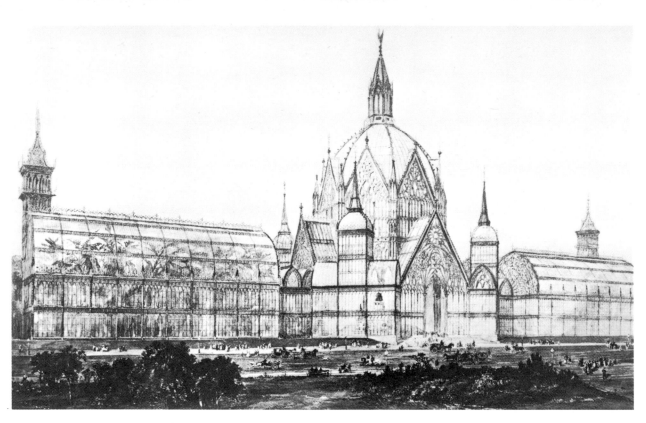

5. Proposed glasshouse to cover the Albert Memorial.
Iron and glass were not solely functionalist materials;
Gothic lightness is here taken to the ultimate

lated into words. In this sense it is possible to parallel architecture
and music: whereas the Romantics sought to express some thought or
poetic idea using music as another form of story-telling, the twentieth
century has largely pursued pure abstract form, sound as it were for
the sake of sound. The same contrast may be found in painting with the
symbolic themes of the Pre-Raphaelites giving way to the increasingly
abstracted images of the twentieth century.

The transition from one form of expression to another is claimed
as a revolutionary stage in the development of art. Subsequently
historians look for indications of this shift in thinking in the products
of the earlier generations and trace the line of development that leads
to the present situation. But this kind of 'pattern-making' can be
misleading (5). Although the early steel-framed office blocks are
seen, rightly, as the ancestors of the twentieth century high-rise
structures, the fact that such Victorian buildings were carefully decorated in accordance with contemporary aesthetic values is often
ignored or, worse still, condemned because decoration conflicts with
the thinking of the Modern Movement. This post-rationalisation has
been responsible for the careless rejection of Victorian architectural
theories and has misled popular opinion with regard to the role of
decoration in architecture.

Architectural ornament should not be seen as a Victorian folly, a
foible of the times. It is, rather, an aspect of architecture which in

6. Early iron-framed building, Glasgow, 1856

past ages has always played a more or less important part in architectural theory. As Adolf Loos observed, where the Greeks were attentive to ornamental details, the Romans concentrated on engineering structures; in the same way where Baroque architecture was extravagant, the Neoclassicism of the eighteenth century was restrained. In principle there has always been this alternating cycle between what may be called the rational and the emotional sides of architecture. Thus the Victorians reacted to the oppressive uniformity of the Georgians and their controlled façades with perfect and regular proportions. Then the twentieth century reacted against the emotional extravagance and picturesque irregularity of the Victorians. And so when we speak of the Functional Tradition we must see it as the obverse of the architectural coin with the Decorative Tradition standing as a clear and tested alternative.

There are many signs that architecture today is at another of these cross-roads where the theories which the past two generations accepted without question are being re-assessed. The fundamental principles of modern architecture are coming under close scrutiny. The idea has been propagated that we build today in the only way that it is possible to build. But if we recognise the swing between the Decorative and the Functional Tradition and recognise the contrast between the two styles and the values that are to be found in both schools of thinking it should be possible to form a more objective assessment of what the future course of architecture could be. It is on this basis that the decorative architecture of the nineteenth century is being reviewed—

15

7. Town centre, Walsall

not in order to establish historical facts but to look at the forms of expression that were used by the Victorians in their buildings and to try to discover what clue they offer to the possible development of our present architecture.

Obviously we are not going to go back to 1900 and carry on from the point at which the Victorians were defeated in the battle against modern functionalism. The Modern Movement may be discredited but, even if it were possible, we should not wish to set back the clock and lose the benefit of the considerable technical skill that has developed this century. It is rather more a question of applying it in a more humane and satisfying direction than the one it has taken up to now.

2 Decoration and the Victorians

The Victorian middle class grew with and represented the new industrial cities of England. Their status and indeed their livelihood was directly related to the development of commerce, factory systems and the production of consumer goods. It was the middle class that invented, manufactured and enjoyed the products of the industrial age. Here was the 'good life' of electricity, education, roads, water supplies, drainage, travel and postal services. Here was the life of Victorian comfort, with gadgets and optical toys, china tea services, embroidery and pommade. There was a deep consciousness that this was a new era of civilisation:

From the beginning of recorded time down to the end of the first quarter of the nineteenth century the means of travel and the means of forwarding messages were very much the same. All that sailing ships and horses and the physical strength of human beings could do for travel and the carrying of messages was done. Then there opened that entirely new era of civilisation when steam and electricity were made to do the work with a speed which would have seemed incredible to a contemporary of Dr Johnson, as well as to a contemporary of Socrates.[*]

This recognition of the change that had taken place during the nineteenth century is further reinforced by another writer:

In certain respects this last century differs more from the age preceding it, than that differed from the Stone Age. We have annihilated time and space as regards travelling, the conveyance of merchandise and verbal intercourse. We have invented machines whose delicate action rivals that of the human fingers and found out substances whose power resembles that of the earthquake. We are enabled to manufacture things that all need, with a rapidity and in an abundance that can only be paralleled in the fairy stories of our youth.[†]

But in spite of all this eagerness for material prosperity and the delight that was felt in the 'magic' of machine production, there were certain aspects of society that were a source of concern for many people; the ugliness, misery and indignity that came with industrialisation could not be overlooked. It was fine to have so much wealth but what was the cost in terms of the quality of human life? And what was the cost to the environment? During the second half of the century there were many who expressed doubts about the condition of industrial England:

---

[*] MacCarthy, Justin. *A History of Our Own Times*, new edition, 1908, Vol. II; p. 389.
[†] Aitcheson, G. *National Association for the Advancement of Art and its Application to Industry*, 1888; p. 142.

[We] may be said to have grown rich by the production and carting of rubbish. This generation has begun to pause in the race, to survey the heaps of gold, to see the disorganisation of society, and to ask itself how society can be re-organised and how wealth can be nobly spent and nobly enjoyed.*

For the Victorians the source of the problem was the separation of man from nature. 'God made the country and man made the town' (Cowper) and man was not making a very good job of his side of it. William Morris and his followers reacted by advocating a rejection of industrial life and a return to medieval craft processes that were long dead. Although he succeeded in improving the general standard of design, Morris's ideas were never a viable alternative for the mass of society who were financially tied to the industrial system. The solution that was most generally adopted, from Ruskin until the turn of the century, was to incorporate nature into city life in some way. In theory it was then possible to gain maximum benefit from industrial society while still keeping in touch with nature. This compromise produced the Royal Parks, the tree-lined streets, the planted gardens in the city squares and towards the turn of the century the garden city suburbs. For the middle class (the working class never had any proper opportunity to interest themselves in the matter) it also resulted in the cultivation of art and taste, naturalistic ornament and decoration and then any ornament and decoration—the Victorian love of beauty and the pursuit of happiness.

The key concept was the creation of a city environment that was a reasonable alternative to country life. The aim was to create an architecture which, although it was artificial, offered the same qualities as nature: variety, individuality, visual interest, colour, delicacy in line and form, in short beauty. The modern dialectic has made us very unsure of the nature of beauty but the Victorians had no such problem. The Futurists were to speak of the beauty of the machine but that was a beauty based on power and fear. For the Victorians beauty had always the connotation of happiness and happiness was associated with what transcended the prosaic and the mundane. 'Nature points out to us that the one gratuitous and harmless delight she offers us is Beauty'†—and so naturalistic ornament and decoration were part of the conscious search for beauty in art, an art that supplemented nature and even surpassed it.

In this way the Victorians hoped to counteract the destructive influence of industrialisation. The further man became removed from nature, the more he sought to recreate it in art. Decoration came to be employed as an aesthetic compensation for the increased complexity, artificiality and restraint with which the new industrialised society had to contend. Art and Beauty were to provide the antidote to Commerce and Industry. One frequently finds such personifications as these in Victorian design: on Holborn viaduct, for instance, there are four statues which symbolise Agriculture, Commerce, Science and Fine Art (8, 9, 10). As Nature retreated in the face of the combined forces of Industry, Commerce and Science, Art came to her rescue claiming the transcendancy of emotional purity and the influence of

* *ibid.*   † ibid.

8. Holborn Viaduct, London, with statues and curious detailing
9. Detail: the bridge has been repainted to good effect
10. Statue personifying Science, Holborn Viaduct

man's highest aspiration to wisdom, knowledge and truth. Every object, therefore, had to represent something and in some way act as a reminder of higher ideals and aspirations. Thus a candle stick was not just a candle holder but a sculpture representing Prometheus stealing fire from the gods, or a phoenix rising out of the flames.

The object itself might well be an industrial product but through decoration it became associated with finer ideals, evoking a response that bore little relationship to the basic function. The Victorians found nothing incompatible in this:

Art as applied to industrial products, means simply the beautifying of the thing made. Whether the result of hand-work or machinery, manufactures are generally associated in the mind with what is useful, art with what is ornamental. Each has a separate and independent existence. We cultivate the useful because of its use; but the better and more spiritual side of our nature finds its affinity in the beautiful. A thing of beauty may have no immediate practical use, a thing of use no appreciable beauty; but in their union the creative genius of man finds its highest and divinest expression, and then only may he, without presumption, regard the work of his hands as 'very good'.*

This theme provided the background to much of Victorian architecture and design. In many respects it was decoration that made architecture meaningful, that made it an art rather than a science. With hindsight it might be said that the Victorian architects were therefore fighting a rearguard action against the engineer whose influence was increasingly apparent in the second half of the century. Up to a point this is true. Ruskin spoke of certain characteristic forms of architectural decoration that were 'venerable or beautiful, but otherwise unnecessary'. Unnecessary to the function, that is, but essential to the nobility and aesthetic quality of the structure.

The theory that justified the widespread use of decoration, however, was not as important as the machinery that made it possible. Art of any kind had always been the privilege of the wealthy few. Victorian technology provided an entirely new situation in which decoration was made available to everyone. Manufactured ornaments were not a Victorian invention. The Georgians had made use of standard mass-produced units: coade-stone surrounds, cast-iron balconies, sash-windows with moulded frames and decorative fanlights. But the range of products was extended with new materials, more complex designs and more sophisticated methods of manufacture. Neither can it be said that picturesque extravaganzas were the sole prerogative of the late nineteenth century—there were the mansions of the early Gothic Revival (like Horace Walpole's Strawberry Hill) and such an imaginative caprice as Brighton Pavilion (11). In the second half of the nineteenth century, however, decorative architecture was produced with a seriousness and studied intensity that was quite different.

The most important factor in the general development of Victorian decorative architecture was the part played by machinery in the manufacture of ornament. While the Georgians had generally employed natural materials like wood and stone, which were worked by

* Forbes Robertson, John, in *Great Industries of Great Britain* 1886, Vol. II; p. 21.

11. Nash's Brighton Pavilion, completed 1827; first of
many seaside pavilions with exuberant decorative
designs

hand, the Victorians made use of terracotta, shaped bricks, tiles and
mosaic which were all manufactured with the assistance of machinery.
An architectural enrichment which would have taken an accomplished
sculptor long hours of careful work could now be cast in terracotta in a
fraction of the time by semi-skilled labour and, of course, for a fraction
of the cost. Most people felt a simple delight in this ability to make such
things with so little effort and marvelled at the work of the decorative
art manufacturers. The novelty of the situation encouraged their
indulgence, in spite of the warnings of men like Walter Crane. 'The
idea of producing art wholesale by steam', he said,* 'is certainly an
extraordinary one. It is very much like printing a misquoted line from
a poet, repeating it page after page and calling the result a book'. The
analogy is rather extreme (though it provides for some interesting
speculations in connection with the work of the Dadaists!) and it leaves
unsolved the perennial problem of how to provide 'art for the millions'

* Crane, Walter. *National Association for the Advancement of Art and its Application to
Industry*, 1888; p. 210.

12. Imperial Hotel, Russell Square (demolished 1966)
Idiosyncratic design in terracotta by C. F. Doll, 1898.

13. Detail

without debasing the coinage. For all that Crane was a socialist, his
ideas on art and craft made no real provision for the aspirations of the
common man. The decorative art manufacturers on the other hand
sold ornaments by the yard and so were able to supply the growing
market with the artistic decorations that everybody wanted.

During the nineteenth century the cities of England developed at an
unprecedented rate—London's population jumped from 1 million to
$4\frac{1}{2}$ million between 1800 and 1900, Manchester's from 100,000 to 550,000
in the same period—and this meant a huge growth in the demand for
every form of building material. It was a matter of practical necessity
to introduce whatever mass-production techniques were available.
There were three forces at work which in combination produced the
main body of Victorian architecture. First the growth of the cities,
secondly this application of industrial manufacturing techniques and
thirdly, as if to compensate for the other two, the use of decoration to
give the building a sense of style and individuality.

This search for individuality is one of the special characteristics of
the Decorative Tradition. Although machines were used to manufacture building materials the design was always directed by the

14. Talbot Rd, London N6; notice 'jewel-like' glass, *c.* 1905

15. Ornamental sculpture on four-roomed house, Lakeside Rd, London W14

16. Victoria Park Rd, Cardiff, with typical decorative
features; *c.* 1905

visual requirements of the scheme. It is to be expected that expensive
buildings would demonstrate a certain originality but the extent of the
idea can best be seen in caricature in the speculative suburban housing
developments that surrounded every town and city in Victorian
Britain. Although these houses were designed in a most mechanical
way each one still succeeded in claiming a separate visual identity
through the addition of different superficial ornaments made by the
decorative art manufacturers. Doulton's, Burmantoft's and J. C.
Edwards sold all kinds of 'architectural enrichment's in terracotta and
different forms of glazed earthenware; Minton's and Maw's made an
extensive range of ceramic tiles, geometric pavements and mosaics;
ironfounders like the Coalbrokedale Co., MacFarlane's of Glasgow or
Barnard, Bishop and Barnard from Norwich produced every conceiv-
able form of decorative metalwork. These firms and hundreds of others
like them were effectively the architects of the suburban terrace
house in the late nineteenth century.

The decorative art manufacturers were the 'architects' since they

17. MacFarlane's of Glasgow, frontispiece of catalogue

provided the styling and above all else styling was the chief characteristic of Victorian architecture. With the exception of the work of a handful of men, domestic architecture was the accumulation of decorative details. An illustration in MacFarlane's catalogue (17) makes this point very clearly. Here is the centre of any town: it is like a puzzle picture, how many uses can be found for ornamental ironwork? The central feature is a drinking fountain for horses and men (long since removed to make way for horseless carriages or to be melted down into guns during the war years). Notice particularly the supporting feet which are cast in the shape of horses' hooves (18), an amusing and typically Victorian piece of decoration. Then there are the lamp posts, balustrades, balconies, window-boxes, window-frames, panelled façades and a public lavatory. Across the street in Victoria Park, which is fenced by cast-iron railings with delicately wrought gates, is a band stand, complete with clock and Gothic pinnacle.

A catalogue from Wilcock's of Leeds offered another wide range of

Nº 27

Circular Horse Trough 6' 6" Diameter, with Lamp Pillar, Bib Valve Drinking Fountain, and Dog Trough. With or without self-acting supply apparatus. Shield with any inscription or device *to order*. Lantern priced separately.

This design is well suited for Street Crossings, Squares, Market Places, Horse Bazaars, &c., as it affords drinking accommodation for a large number of horses and drivers, and effectively lights a wide space, with the least possible obstruction to the other traffic.

SCALE

18. Water trough for men, horses and dogs, MacFarlane's

27

DESIGNED BY MAURICE B. ADAMS A·R·I·B·A·

DOMESTIC·WINDOWS·IN·CONSTRUCTIVE·FAÏENCE· MADE·BY·WILCOCK·&·CO· BURMANTOFTS, LEEDS·

19/20. Catalogues of terracotta and architectural faience, by Wilcock & Co., Burmantofts, Leeds; 1882

details in terracotta and constructional faience (19, 20). These designs for windows, porches and decorative string courses had only to be ordered, so many of each type, and they would be delivered to the site ready for the builder. Another catalogue provided designs in stained and painted glass, another supplied information about various shaped and coloured roofing tiles. A letter to Maw & Co. of Ironbridge Gorge and they would send their latest pattern book—a few yards of geometric pavement, perhaps, a panel of tiles inside the porch, or even a custom-made mosaic with the relevant names and dates. The quantity and the quality of the decoration depended on the class of building and its position on the architectural ladder. These mass-produced ornaments that were used so extensively in suburban terraces imitated the more elaborate buildings that can be found in the city centre with their correspondingly more elaborate decoration. It was factory production that made possible the proliferation of such ornaments to every class of building.

The role of the machine in art and design had long been a matter for debate. Walter Crane might scoff at the idea of mass-producing ornaments but in the eyes of most people a building without decoration was nothing, it was naked, an undressed and rude structure. To parallel Crane's analogy that machine-made decoration was like an endlessly misquoted line, there were others who pointed out that a poem without

PORCHES
EXECUTED·IN·TERRA·COTTA
AND·BURMANTOFTS·FAÏENCE
BY·WILCOCK·AND·C?·LEEDS·
— DESIGNED · BY —
MAURICE B.ADAMS A.R.I.B.A.ARCⁿ

A·GARDEN·PORCH·

A·Closed·Porch·

An Open Porch

adjectives and adverbs would be no poem at all, just a collection of words without colour or lyricism. By the same token architecture without ornament was ungracious and vulgar, without refinement or sophistication. The advocates of simplicity were to have their way eventually but in the Victorian heyday they were ignored as everybody revelled in the opportunity that the machine provided for architectural decoration that was universally available for the first time.

3 The Function of Decoration

Having spoken of the opposition between the Functional and Decorative Traditions it is necessary to stress again the point that this is a distinction that would never have been made in the nineteenth century. It is only the historian who seeks to make such neat delineations. To the Victorians, architectural decoration had a very clear *function* within the overall concept of architectural theory. Some of the reasons for the Victorian love of decoration have been discussed, but as well as the general delight in any kind of ornamentation it was used as a definite expression of purpose and meaning in architecture. While modern architecture wanted to create the 'anonymous products of a uniform language' and so reflect the uniform goals of society, the Victorians sought to emphasise individuality and the hierarchical structure within society. Ornament was not only an expression of use but also of status.

There was a language of symbols and styles that reflected the established values of society. By inference, the use of a certain form of ornament gave a building the status that the ornament represented. Gothic carvings symbolised Gothic architecture and medieval culture; thus to use Gothic ornament in the nineteenth century was to declare a congruency of ideas between the two separate ages. At a time when the Industrial Revolution was bringing about such sweeping changes in every walk of life, this gave a symbolic cohesion to society. Architectural decoration played an important part in maintaining the stability of the community. This can best be seen in the forms of ornamentation used in public buildings, though the process was reflected throughout the whole range of building types.

In the middle decades of the century there was rivalry between the exponents of Gothic and Classical architecture that has been well documented under the title 'The Battle of the Styles'. While men like Ruskin and Pugin were of the opinion that Gothic* could supply the best style to fit any occasion, others like Wilkins, Smirke and Nash had chosen to follow Classical precedents. The battle was to be resolved during the 1860s with what Kerr called 'latitudinarianism' which suggested that any and all styles should be used as the situation demanded. Generally speaking, neo-Gothic architecture came within

* A distinction is usually made between the Gothic Revival of the late eighteenth century, neo-Gothic which was early Victorian and mainly ecclesiastical and commercial Gothic which was a free adaptation of the style.

the province of the church and neo-Classical forms were essentially secular.

When an architect designed in the Gothic style, then, he aligned his work with that of the medieval master builders who created the churches and cathedrals of Western Europe. This had an obvious connection with the thinking of the Oxford Movement and the Tractarians (1833–41) and thus with the reassertion of High Church Catholicism. The work of Pugin was particularly important in this respect and his books like *The True Principles of Pointed or Christian Architecture* (1841) were an expression of deep religious conviction. Pugin was obsessively Gothic and the ornaments that he used on his buildings were vital expressions of his belief. One of the objections to the Gothic style came from non-conformists and Low Church clergy who felt that the lavish decorations were an unnecessary expense. Thus ecclesiastical architecture in the Gothic style expressed particular religious values. This situation might be examined more closely by looking at the exact parentage of the styles that were used, whether Early English, Decorated or Perpendicular; in his book on the Gothic Revival (1872), Charles Eastlake gave a list of all important churches built in the past fifty years and the dates of their inherited styles.

Pugin's example was followed, perhaps with less intensity, by many others and the outward forms of Gothic came to symbolise not just a kind of christian moral rearmament but the more general values of the Pre-Renaissance. One of the functions of Gothic ornament was to suggest the moral purity of the age and the virtues of an education based on religion and christian philosophy. Schools and colleges were built in the neo-Gothic style and Gothic ornament was used to symbolise a romantic image of 'cloistered learning'. This was particularly significant for the Victorians since it paralleled the founding of the universities and the introduction of general schooling after the Education Act of 1870.

In England the original Gothic period finally came to a close with the Reformation. For more than a hundred years the Renaissance had brought increasing conflict between Church and State; as Gothic architecture had symbolised the primacy of the Church, so Classical architecture became the symbol of the State. Here again, in the nineteenth century, the style was used because of its associations. One of the functions of neo-Classical ornaments was to express the idea of civic dignity. Monumental sculpture, imposing pillared façades, classical pediments and friezes spoke of the grandeur of Victorian empire and compared it, metaphorically, with the splendour that was Rome. The Classical style was predominantly used for government buildings, town halls, banks and similar institutions (like the clubs in Pall Mall and St James's). It is significant that in the competition for the new Whitehall buildings (1857), Palmerston eventually gave a directive that Scott should design in the Classical rather than the Gothic Style.

Commercial buildings often borrowed the dignity of an institution by using the same forms of ornament and so evoking the same respect. These 'monuments of commerce', the smaller banks, insurance

21. Imperial Hotel, Henley-on-Thames; *c.* 1885

offices and exchanges* had to be both functional and grand. In the first age of office building it was impossible to use the extravagant internal spaces of Palladian architecture, yet the clients still wished to pretend to the grand Medicean ideals of Victorian business. So external ornament was deliberately employed to suggest an assumed magnificence

* see Taylor, Nicholas, *Monuments of Commerce*; 1968.

that properly speaking was bogus. This was often the function of decoration, to pretend that a building was something better than it was, a pretence that later brought the accusation that image took precedence over substance.

In the late decades of the nineteenth century, this neo-Classical dignity gave way to the search for individuality. As the real power of commerce was transferred from the aristocracy to the middle class more emphasis was placed on originality. Ornament was used to express the personality of an individual building rather than confirm its uniformity with the old establishment as the Classical styles did. Half-timbered buildings with leaded windows, for instance, became a symbol of bourgeois respectability. With the implication of burgher reliability, this mock Elizabethan style might be used for provincial banks (like the one in the market square at Wantage) and hotels (21). Classical and Gothic styles were freely adapted to novel ornamental forms and were often loosely combined in an effort to find a new and dramatic visual effect.

Architectural decoration was used to attract attention and so act as a kind of advertising. This can be seen in stores like Harrods' in Knightsbridge with its distinctive terracotta façade. There is no particular style here, but the accumulation of ornamental detailwork produced a building that is quite unmistakable. In the same way, the half-timbering and painted ornaments on the front of Liberty's, Great Marlborough Street, London, were designed to attract attention. With the Classical uniformity of Nash's work in Regent Street nearby this was a daring piece of decorative architecture. It might be said, perhaps, that such buildings served only to show the necessity for the balanced serenity of a uniform style such as Nash employed. But the Victorians became a little more adventurous and they had grown tired of such things. They wanted novelty, buildings that were going to vaunt themselves and catch the eye of the public. The decorative façade of Liberty's fits in extraordinarily well with the present image of neighbouring Carnaby Street.

Another example of ornamental design that provides individuality for commercial premises can be seen at the Mayfair shop of Thos Goode's. Built in 1876, this brick building was a typical product of the Aesthetic Movement. It is not easy to see any coherent form in the structure. The architect seems to have applied most of his effort in obtaining a striking effect with the ornaments and decorations. There are niches on the front of the building for large vases (then, as now, the shop sold fine china and glass), the ribs of the chimney-stacks run right up the side of the building developing into giant sunflowers near the top; on another side there are two large dolphins cast in brick. Iron railings run around the building at first floor level with ornamental sunflowers; on one wall, positioned in an arbitrary way it seems, there is a brick panel showing a potter working at his wheel (72). On the same side of the building, at street level, there are panels of decorative tilework within stuccoed arches. These murals are in the Japanese style with pictures of birds, butterflies and blossom branches (22, 23, 24). In themselves these panels are very fine; the delicacy of the paint-

22. Thos Goode's, South St, Mayfair, London; 1876

ing and the Japanese flavour may have had some justifiable relationship with the shop and the goods it had for sale at that time. But in a strictly architectural sense the building lacks any proper cohesion and the ornaments are merely applied wherever convenient.

That, at least, is the criticism at one level. But the Victorians were not particularly concerned with the correctness of proportion and form. They often did not look for the unity of a building, but saw it rather as an assemblage of parts each of which was to be interesting and visually attractive in itself. And there is something in this. In towns there is rarely an opportunity to see the complete building. Because of the angle of vision of the eye and the viewing distance available we see parts of a building separately; this is particularly true of the small streets in Mayfair. Grosvenor Square, of course, is a different matter. So the exterior of Goode's was designed with a number of different decorative features that would attract attention wherever the viewer stood in relation to the building. Each piece of ornamental-work was designed in relation to the position it was to occupy on the building and less attention was paid to their overall relationship one to another.

This points clearly to the fact that one of the primary functions of decoration in commercial buildings was to capture the attention of a potential customer. But decoration also had an interpretive function. As the Gothic spire announced the position of a church and the windows and carvings were lessons to the congregation, so the decorations first drew one's attention and then, through the use of familiar symbols, conveyed some essential information. Thus the Victorian aes-

23/24. Tile panels in Japanese style which here symbolised the refined 'good taste' of the goods for sale

thete would instantly realise that here was a shop for those of refined taste—the sunflowers made that clear in the popular idiom. Unmistakably this was a china shop, why otherwise would there be two large ornamental pots outside? And if those were not seen then the

25. Rising Sun, Tottenham Court Rd, London 1897

picture of a potter at work should make the matter quite clear. But more especially, here was a shop selling Japanese goods, china and porcelain whose delicacy and refinement could be equated with that of the tile murals on the side of the building. One further point about the decoration of commercial buildings, something that is second nature in contemporary advertising: the more impressive the architectural ornaments were, the more likely that the shop would be remembered. Goode's could always be known by the beauty of their tilework, just as Harrods' would always be familiar by virtue of the colour, pattern and outline of the terracotta façade. Thus, in the nineteenth century, architecture was as much a part of the company housestyle as graphics are today.

This kind of identification through ornamental symbols is apparent in other types of building. The neo-Classical details in domestic architecture, from Lowndes Square to Kensington, denoted upper

26. Alms-houses in domestic Gothic style, Greenwich,
London; 1884

middle-class respectability. The consistency of style in area developments affirmed a certain social standard. Those grand terraces in
Belgravia, built by Cubitt in the 1830s, were imitated in style if not in
quality by a generation of other developers. The stuccoed façades, the
Classical columns in the porch, the ornamental window-box railings
and the small pediments over windows all became part of the standard
vocabulary of ornament from the Kensington garden-squares to the
'Italianate villas' in Belsize Park. Again it was a case of Classical
styling lending a dignity and uniformity to buildings.

Up until the mid 1860s most city houses were built on similar lines
to those evolved by the Regency developers: simple unornamented
brick terraces for the working class and these stuccoed villas with
vaguely Classical details for the wealthier householder. One type of
building that is an interesting exception is the alms-house which
often inclined towards Gothic, if for no better reason than that they
were usually privately endowed and so more elaborate decoration was
financially possible (26). Alms-houses also had some association with
the Middle Ages and so neo-Gothic ornament was thought to be suitable. During the last three decades of the century, however, the style of
domestic architecture changed considerably. This was largely under
the influence of the Aesthetic Movement when decoration became a
matter of status and even the meanest dwelling made some pretension
to sophistication.

It is not so easy to speak of the function of decoration in domestic
architecture, though ornaments were used generally to obtain individuality and novelty, reflecting at a lower octave the larger architectural schemes of the day. Victorian housing estates usually were
built by a lower school of designers, not the well known architects

27. Montrose Villas, East Finchley, London; 1883

whose work figures in the history books. In layout and space allocation there was little change throughout the nineteenth century, but the changes in popular taste can be traced in the minor points of decoration. These decorations were bought from the catalogues of the decorative art manufacturers. Plans might be taken from a magazine like *The Illustrated Carpenter and Builder*, tiles bought from Minton's or Maw's, iron railings from Macfarlane's, terracotta ornaments from Doulton's or Burmantoft's and so on. The various parts had only to be assembled in the right order and another bijou residence was created.

Designing a building in this way shows the worst aspect of the Decorative Tradition. But many of the speculative housing schemes were thought out on this basis. Even admitting their shortcomings, the mechanical designs have a quality that is missing from the modern equivalent. Through the use of different decorative details they achieved an interest and individuality that is totally lacking in contemporary council estates or suburban housing. A direct comparison would be difficult and probably unjust, but look at Montrose Villas in East Finchley (27, 28) by way of an example. These cottages are the most basic type of two-up-two-down and there is hardly any need for the floor plan it is so simple and standard. But each doorway was given a different capital on the miniature columns, a stylised head, a swag of fruit or a wreath of leaves and flowers. Between the windows is a similar casting with a floral design or the name of the street. Some of the houses still have the original coloured glass lights over the doorway with the house number. The skyline presents similar variations with shaped chimney-pots and curly terracotta ridge tiles: each roof is

28. Details. Each house has minor variations providing individuality

topped with a pinnacle with a different design, made in iron or terra-cotta.

In Montrose Villas the decoration was constrained by economic factors. The amount and variety of the ornament in any speculative scheme was limited by the budget and the class of the property. And so the larger detached houses that were built around Hampstead or Belsize Park, for instance, show much more individuality and cor-

29. Eton Avenue, London NW3; *c.* 1880.

respondingly more elaborate details (29). The pinnacles are no longer
small knobs of terracotta but grotesque dragons and bizarre monsters.
Beneath the window there is not just a single plaque but a frieze of
brickwork with sunflower patterns. Each of the chimney-pots is
curiously moulded and sculpted, unlike the simpler thrown forms of
Montrose Villas. These streets of houses such as Eton Avenue are
similar in style but completely individual in appearance. This quality
of separate visual character in combination with the use of factory-
made materials is significant. This was the new architecture of the
Victorian middle class: mass produced and yet given a sense of identity
and individuality through the application of ornament and decoration.

In the end this kind of ornamentation became rather self-defeating.
When every terrace house made the same appeal for attention the small
variations in detail became almost meaningless in the context of the
jumble of bits of decoration. There is little to justify these excesses
when they are judged by the yardstick of good architectural taste. And

yet there is no doubt that for better or worse the owners themselves derived a great deal of pleasure and satisfaction from these small ornaments. In the last resort the function of decoration is to make people happy. There is no doubt that there was, and still is, a good deal of snobbery attached to architecture. Not everybody can live in a castle and so it was necessary to make the most of what was available. In this 'deep pit of speculative building' there were plenty of architectural disasters, but even if these trivial ornaments could show at a glance the exact social status and income of the householder that should not detract from their essential value. It is easy to laugh at the foibles of the Victorian middle class, as exemplified by Mr Pooter in *The Diary of a Nobody*, but he was a product of his age and his values were those taught to him by society. It was the same in architecture. However misguided some of their work may appear, the underlying principle in all decorative Victorian architecture was the pursuit of beauty.

4 Ornamental Forms

In their search for beauty in architecture, the Victorians were constantly looking for precedents to justify their use of ornament and to act as examples to imitate and for inspiration. Magazines on art and architecture (like the *Art Journal* and the *Builder*) carried regular articles on historical subjects which encouraged and justified the eclecticism that was so characteristic of the nineteenth century. Any designer who was short of an idea had only to open a magazine to find inspiration and guidance from historical examples. This process was reinforced by a library of books on architectural decoration and style which could be directly copied. With a minimum of text and clear detail drawings, they provided an encyclopedia of ornamental forms. 'A wealthy community always erects decorated buildings', said Dresser in the introduction to his *Studies in Design* (1874–6) and acting on this premise he found little need for further comment but simply supplied examples of his work for the guidance of his imitators. Other books such as J. O'Kane's *Detail Ornament*, published in New York in 1882, or *Art and Work* by Owen Davis (1885) followed the same format.

Those who found the old styles of Western Europe a little unadventurous might refer to textbooks like Thomas Cutler's *A Grammar of Japanese Ornament and Design* (1880). For, as Britain expanded her economy abroad with trade and empire, so too she traded the superficial forms of decorative architecture and design. Little attempt was made to understand properly either the meaning or purpose of such foreign styles. The emphasis was on novelty and the visual qualities of the decoration. A good image was always considered more important than a cleverly made joint or a new form of construction. For the Victorians there was a clear distinction between Art and Science; architectural ornament that was 'artistic' took little account of building technology.

The situation was encouraged by the introduction of art education. At the Great Exhibition of 1851, Britain's inferiority in artistic manufactures had been made very apparent:

... it did not take long to ascertain that the cause was the neglect of art education among the people, while the continental artisans were taught with the greatest care and familiarised from their youth with *the choicest productions of ancient and modern art*. It was conceded that the art schools and museums of France exercised a great influence upon the manufactures of that country. England saw that to compete with such a rival great efforts must be made and that the people must be educated.*

The result was that art schools were set up, eventually throughout the country. Here students were taught to imitate styles with an alarming accuracy. Government examinations tested a pupil's ability to reproduce the details of acceptable ornament but there was little encouragement to show any real initiative. And there were further books written for students, like Owen Carter's *On Designing Tiles* or James Ward's *Elementary Principles of Ornament* (a textbook for students taking Third Grade government exams, consisting of lectures given at the Macclesfield School of Art) which added to the flow of information. Education there was and education with a vengeance. With a regional emphasis (pottery for North Staffordshire, textiles for the spinning towns) these schools taught the artists and designers who were to create the popular ornamental art of the late nineteenth century.

So a generation of designers was born who had been weaned on Ruskin and the Battle of the Styles, who were party to the popular pursuit of decoration and ornament, who were conversant with the Japanese taste of the period as well as the history of a host of other historical styles, and who were free from all constraint and inhibition. They used all forms of decoration with an urbane assurance, not only for smart buildings in the middle of the town but in speculative housing schemes on the outer limits of industrial cities. As A. E. Street commented in his review of Victorian architecture:

The purist of an earlier [or a later] day would be shocked at the freedom with which the raw material of style is handled now, while the stickler for an ethical basis in architecture would hold up his hands aloft to see the cheerful eclecticism with which the designer today skips from century to century, or stands with his feet wide apart while the ages roll between.†

Before looking at the forms of Victorian ornament it is necessary to say something about this term 'eclectic'. Properly speaking it refers to a school of thinking that selects such doctrines as are convenient or pleasing from other philosophies; an eclectic borrows freely from various sources, untroubled by the scruples of the purist who seeks consistency and originality in thinking. In architectural terms this can be seen as an expression of uncertainty, when the lack of a clearly discernible style that is universally acceptable encourages the designer to imitate the work of other periods and cultures. The Victorian architects, therefore, were eclectic because they used bits of Classical design, bits of Gothic, they borrowed from the Japanese, they imitated the Dutch and so on. They selected those aspects of foreign styles that appealed and bent them to their own purposes. Since before the time of Street and through to the present day, the Victorians have been upbraided for this eclecticism and the word has always been used in a perjorative sense. But to say that nineteenth century ornament was eclectic is a quite inadequate dismissal.

It has been stressed that the chief quality of Victorian architecture

* Blake, William P. *Ceramic Art*: A Report on Pottery, Porcelain Tiles, Terracotta and Brick; New York, 1875.
† Street, A. E. 'Architecture in the Victorian Era', *Architectural Review*, April 1901.

was the emphasis that was placed on the visual impact of the building and its symbolic association. If we can accept that a Dutch building is a happy expression of Holland, then what prevents us from taking pleasure, by association, in buildings that imitate the Dutch like Ernest George's work in Collingham and Harrington Gardens, London (1882)? If we find Japanese design interesting and attractive, then why not make use of it to produce interesting and attractive decoration? The answers lie, to some extent, in how this was done. If a style was employed consistently then it became acceptable as a style. Unfortunately, several of the decorative art manufacturers and many of the less educated architects were so eager to obtain some kind of individuality for their work that they employed any available decorative form, irrespective of its suitability or origin.

There were those who strongly advocated the adoption of one particular style, like Ruskin and Pugin, the champions of the Gothic Revival which they said was the only true national style in English architecture. There were their opponents in the Battle of the Styles who called for a universal form of Classical building, based on the teachings of Vitruvius. Then there were men like Philip Webb, Morris and Voysey who dismissed style *per se* and concentrated on the 'suitable' use of building materials. Each school of thought believed itself to be entirely right and failing to reach any general agreement they further encouraged eclecticism.

It was generally agreed that ornament was not style, although there was a tendency to regard the accumulation of ornamental details as an expression of style. This was a point that was laboured by Ruskin. He spoke of the necessity for a unified expression of all forms of art that should find its most complete statement in architecture.* He had it constantly in his mind that architecture should express some unifying concept that would demonstrate man's harmonious relationship with nature. This he found in the architecture of the pre-Renaissance; in the Gothic churches and cathedrals of Western Europe. In order to substantiate his support of Gothic architecture he made an analysis of the style, always relating his thinking to the central premise that man's work should reflect God and Nature. In *The Stones of Venice* (first published 1853), he states the axiom that:

The proper material of ornament will be whatever God has created; and its proper treatment, that which seems in accordance with or symbolic of his laws.†

Thus Ruskin was able to list the possible sources for ornamental subjects, stating, defiantly, that 'the reader may be assured that no effort has ever been successful to draw elements of beauty from any

* Eastlake says of him:
But Mr Ruskin's taste for art was a comprehensive one. He learnt at an early age that painting, sculpture and architecture are intimately associated, not merely in their history, but in their practice, and in the fundamental principles that regulate their respective styles. . . . Mr Ruskin looked around him at the modern architecture of England and saw that it not only did not realise this ideal but it was diametrically opposed to it. He found the majority of his countrymen profoundly indifferent to the art [of architecture] or interested in it chiefly as antiquarians and pedants.—Eastlake, Charles, *A History of the Gothic Revival*, 1872; Victorian library edition, 1970; p. 264–5.
† Ruskin, John, *Stones of Venice*, Complete Works; 1903; Vol. IX; p. 264–5.

other sources than these'.* This list is important since it was the theoretical foundation for the decorative art of Victorian architecture and with such modifications as were convenient it was a catalogue of possible ornament for the rest of the century:

(I) Abstract Lines: these are to be taken from natural objects, notably rock formations and landscape contours.

(II) Forms of the Earth: by this Ruskin meant crystals and crystalline geometry, from which were derived such Gothic mouldings as 'dog tooth' ornament.

(III) Forms of Water: symbolically this can be expressed as 'an undulating thing with fish in it', waves.

(IV) Forms of Fire: the radiating sun is most important, though any flames and rays of light are acceptable.

(v) Forms of the Air: it is not easy to represent air and so it is of little use for ornament! However, clouds offer some possibilities.

(VI) Shells: the image of a crab 'is delightful as grotesque', but with scallops, cockles and so on there are many opportunities to create pleasing effects and show the delight of natural geometry.

(VII) Fish: these are of 'great value' as ornamental subjects, presumably to be combined with forms of water.

(VIII) Reptiles and Insects: an interesting combination of beauty and horror is produced here, which had a strange fascination for the Victorians.

(IX) Vegetation I: this category includes what Ruskin called 'stems' and 'trunks'—the self-supporting plant structures.

(x) Vegetation II: leaves, foliage and flowers; Ruskin notes that 'where nothing else can be used for ornament, vegetation may; vegetation in any form, however fragmentary, however abstracted'.

(XI) Birds: a favourite subject with their perfect and simple grace.

(XII) Mammalian Animals and Man: this category is extremely large. In the first instance both animals and man could be depicted in their natural state, though elsewhere Ruskin gave further indications as to how man might be represented.

This list of ornamental subjects closely equates with the forms of Gothic detail. Ruskin, for instance, compared the pointed Gothic arch to the shape of leaves and on the occasion of a lecture that he gave in Edinburgh he railed against the vulgarity of rectangular window frames that were so common there. Although the lintel is the simplest way of bridging an opening it is also the least imaginative and according to the principles of natural structure it is the least economical. In Edinburgh there was an abundance of good building stone, why, he asked, was it not being used creatively? In other districts terracotta was used instead of stone but the same principles applied. In fact, it was easier to construct pointed arches in terracotta since the material was stronger in compression than in tension. Of course, terracotta was unacceptable to Ruskin since it was not a natural material. It was rarely possible to adhere strictly to all his rulings. Another example is the use of ornamental sculpture such as reptiles

* Ibid, p. 282.

30. Strathray Gardens, London NW3; *c.* 1880

and monsters, which Ruskin said should be made in stone but were commonly moulded in terracotta or cast in metal. If architectural ornaments were to be produced in any quantity it was essential to use factory production techniques.

In making this list of ornamental subjects, Ruskin was more intent on showing the relationship between architectural decoration and nature than he was in widening the range of ornamental forms. His classification suffers from a self-conscious attempt to include every possible level of natural form, hence his four categories Earth, Water, Fire and Air which have little practical value or relevance. In an attempt to make a classification of Victorian decoration, Ruskin's list of twelve subjects has been reduced to six: abstract lines, geometric shapes, vegetation, animal forms, mythical subjects, human

31. Chimney pot, Belsize Park Gardens, London NW3;
c. 1865

scenes and stories. Necessarily these groups are still artificial since they take no account of the different styles that developed. But in a way this has a neat relationship with the eclecticism of the period since the subject areas of each style are dealt with collectively.

Abstract Lines

The actual form of the building can be, in itself, ornamental. The flowing lines of the structure, the arc of the roof, the domes and spires are all essentially developed from abstract lines. According to Ruskin these shapes should be taken from nature and copied from the contours of the landscape. This would guarantee a harmonious relationship between the building and its various parts, and the whole and its environment. Although some of the Gothic forms look as if they might have been inspired in this way (the Alpine peaks would have served well), it is doubtful whether Ruskin actually persuaded many architects to go out and sketch natural forms before they started designing.

Apart from this rather dubious connection, it is fair to say that the Victorians took great pains to make every aspect of a building attractive and except where it was expedient to have straight lines and a flat surface, they preferred to use curves. All the openings in a building could be arched, the gables were stepped and scooped after the style of the Dutch (30), columns were fluted with spiralling Ionic capitals, pillars were moulded and topped with urns and globes and walls were rounded off with shaped cappings. Chimney pots were waisted and decorated (31) and in the seventies and eighties they became a particular feature of the building with ribs of curling patterns in the Queen Anne style.

Where modern architecture is rectangular, Victorian architecture was curvilinear. This was particularly true of applied ornament which was non-structural. The cast iron balconies were delicately bowed with an abstract pattern of curves repeated in each strut and panel; spiral staircases led down into the garden. Wrought iron was drawn into ornamental motifs (32) especially towards the end of the century when English Art Nouveau designers discovered the real joy of abstract linear form. Coloured glass was worked into fantastic shapes that only bore the faintest resemblance to some exotic tropical flower (107). Abstract linear forms flowed easily in brick and terracotta panels as, for instance, in Pont Street, London (33).

It is often difficult to distinguish between decorative forms that are non-representational and representational patterns that are abstracted to such an extent that they are barely recognisable. Abstract floral motifs will be dealt with later, but it should be said that many of the vignettes that were used in decoration were loosely based on organic forms. This connection can be seen in the products of the Arts and Crafts Movement with their small decorative details, like the rustic door hinges that Voysey designed.

32. Ornamental wrought iron gas-lamp bracket, *c.* 1900

33. Pont St 'dutch' style brick decoration, London
SW1; *c.* 1885

Finally it might help to define this area of decoration by contrast—
if the set square were to be the symbol of modern architecture, then
french curves would represent the nineteenth century!

Geometric Shapes

Some of the remarks made about abstract lines apply equally to geometric shapes, inasmuch as the form of the building was often geometrical. The decorative effect of this can be seen in the repetition of a well-proportioned terrace house, with triangular gables, rectangular windows and so on. However, it must be admitted that proportional geometry was not the strong point of Victorian architecture and few Victorian terraces were as well proportioned as their Georgian predecessors. Since the Victorians liked curvilinear forms it is to be expected that geometrical ornaments were limited to those materials that dictated their own form by virtue of the material and the production process: bricks, roof tiles and slates and decorative ceramic tiles are notable examples.

A brick is a brick and in order to be useful as a building material it has to be regular in size and shape. Ornamental forms could be made by shaping the surface (see next chapter) but it was more normal to create decorative patterns through the symmetrical repetition of the courses, using special bonds. The same is true of slates and tiles (63).

Ceramic tiles also have regular dimensions and six-inch square tiles, in particular, often had a geometric pattern either as a single unit or when built up into a surface with four or sixteen tiles, although floral patterns were more common. Certainly the most extensive use of ornamental geometry was for floor tiles. Geometric pavements, as they were called, were constructed of small sections of tiles (usually triangular), with different colours, which were used to compose a geometrical pattern. They were very popular in all classes of building for paths, porches, hallways and conservatories (84). Less delicate, though working on the same principle, tiles with an indented pattern were used for pavements and streets (34), just as sets and cobbles were in an earlier age. Unfortunately these have been replaced in almost all cases by tarmac and concrete slabs. The latter point to the importance of geometrical decoration since, by virtue of their size, colour and texture they fail to provide any visual interest whatsoever.

Vegetation

Decorative subjects that were taken from vegetable forms were used more generally than any other class of ornament. In the second half of the nineteenth century there were very few buildings that did not have some kind of decoration that was based on flowers, leaves or stylised plant structures. These designs were usually one of three kinds. They might be a repeating pattern of some single abstracted motif, a pictorial representation of some stylised vegetable form, or a floral or leaf design that was used as a unifying element in a more general design.

Abstracted floral motifs were often used for tiles and decorative brick inserts (36, 37). Symmetrical patterns, based on a four, five or six inch square were taken from flowers with a regular geometry such as sunflowers, dahlias or dog-roses. Few of these designs can be recognised as any particular plant however, and it was quite usual to devise a pattern that was representative of flowers in general, without

34. Blue glazed paving tiles, Yarm, Yorkshire

35. Coal hole covers with simple but attractive patterns

36/37. Decorative brick inserts in wall, Worcester, in pillar, North London

regard for botanical accuracy. Leaf patterns were worked in the same way, not in the hope of creating an overall effect of vegetation, rather as a symbolic image of nature. Because of the scale of these images they served as little more than surface pattern that offered visual relief on a flat wall surface. Similar designs were often used for iron railings, either as a repeating unit for each strut, an embellishment at intervals along the top or as a corner-piece to a balcony (38).

This kind of ornament was distinctly Victorian. While there is nothing unique about the idea of breaking up a surface by introducing a different element at intervals, only the Victorians took such pains to make these small units so decorative. The Georgians used stone copings, some regional styles had flint inserts, a modern architect might use panels of colour, but the Victorians made use of every opportunity to introduce some 'artistic' embellishment that demonstrated both their love of nature and the delight they felt in being able to produce such complexity with so little effort.

In architectural decoration, plants and flowers were rarely drawn with any great accuracy. Designers did not look for an exact naturalism in their work, it was their task to interpret the form into a stylised picture that would represent the idea of nature rather than copy it. Ceramic tiles often had floral designs, roses, violets or chrysanthemums growing in pots, but these were regularised to the shape of the panel and simplified to take account of the manufacturing process (85). The same is true of the larger terracotta panels (39), where flowers, shrubs and even trees might be used in a stylised form. Leaves and fruit were sometimes worked in quite a realistic way, around the capital of a column or as a wall panel beneath a window (28, 40). In the seventies and eighties, lilies and sunflowers were the symbols of the Aesthetic Movement and they were used for architectural ornament of every kind (41).

38. Cast iron balcony, Old Brompton Rd, London *c*. 1875
39. Terracotta panel, S. Wales Institute of Engineers,
Cardiff; 1893

At about the same time, Japanese art became popular in Britain and
this provided a new approach to ornamental design. The style of
drawing encouraged a free interpretation of exotic flowers, grasses
and bamboos. But the Japanese influence was most strongly felt in
interior design where, in many households, it became fashionable to
have a 'Japanese room'. There were fewer possibilities for architectural
decoration (since attention was paid only to the superficial forms of
the style), although ceramic murals provided a good medium for
two-dimensional design (23, 24).

Most ornaments in this category of vegetable forms were in low
relief. With the exception of metal, it was impossible to create such
delicate structures as nature in the materials available for building.

40. Sculpted brick panels, Earls Court Sq, London

41. Sculpted brick, Belsize Avenue, London NW3; *c.* 1880

Vegetation was used generally to cover a plain surface. It was ideal for flourishes and vignettes and as a kind of pictorial shading within an area of decoration (42). Most of the cusps and mouldings, the borders and trims that surround windows and frame ornamental panels, were derived from natural forms. Podgy cherubs trailed streams of foliage, terracotta heads were couched in a rosette of leaves. At least one thing that Ruskin said was taken to heart by the Victorian decorative art manufacturers:

Where nothing else can be used for ornament, vegetation may; vegetation in any form, however fragmentary, however abstracted.*

Animals

While vegetation might be abstracted as ornamental motifs, animals had to be represented with a fair degree of accuracy. Even fictitious monsters (see next section) had to be given a certain verisimilitude. Whether bird, fish or mammal, ornamental animals are always recog-

* Ruskin; op. cit.

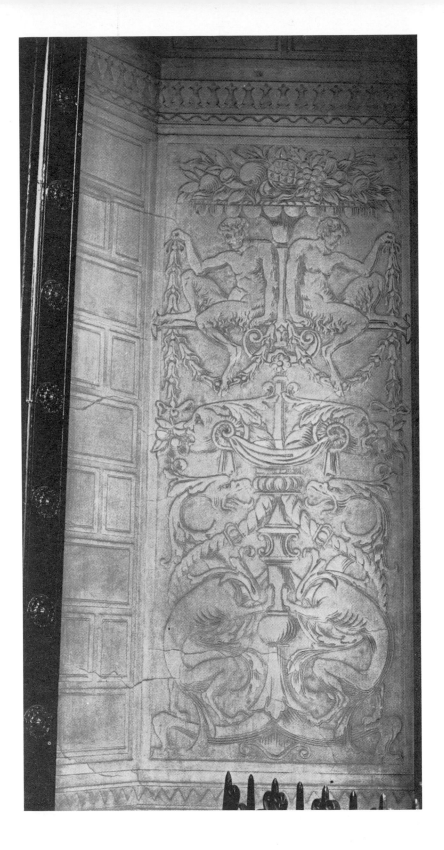

42. Decorative plasterwork in porch, Palace Gate, London W8

43. Buff terracotta sculptures, Gloucester; 1898

44. Cast iron lamp post, Archway, North London; 1897

nisable and usually formed a complete image in themselves. Sculpted lions, dogs and cats were perched on the side of buildings (43) and in Oxford Street, London, there are three beavers sitting on a roof watching the buses going by. Horses, usually with a famous rider astride their back, were commonly used in monumental sculpture, as in Trafalgar Square, where the British lion also guards Nelson's column. Fish of an indeterminate species coil around lamp posts (44) and on the side of Thos Goode's premises in Mayfair giant dolphins cut in brick swim up towards the chimneys. With the exception of monumental work, animals were used in this way to create surprise and humour.

Animals appear, as one might expect, in pictorial ornament: the cows of the Crouch Hill dairy, for example (122, 123, p. 115ff.), and the cod at Scott's Emulsion (127, p. 118ff.). The Japanese influence made tropical birds a popular subject and brightly coloured parrots sat on slender branches with their tail feathers trailing in a delicate curve (23). The aesthetic peacock spreads it plumes in terracotta over a doorway in Great Smith Street, Victoria. In Hammersmith a mosaic panel advertised the Swan Hotel (46) with a picture of the bird swimming among rushes and water lilies.

A good many more examples might be given though in each case the animals were used in the same way, as an image that enlivened the visual impression of the building. This form of ornament was not usually related to the structure in any way and served only to delight the passer-by.

Mythological Subjects
Many of the terracotta and brick sculptures that decorated Victorian buildings were of indeterminate origin: partly natural, partly imagi-

45. Detail of Thos Goode's, Mayfair: tile plaque, 1876

46. Swan Hotel, Hammersmith, London, mosaic picture; 1901

47. Tiled mural, Poole docks

nary and in part mythological creatures. Encrusted on the façade like vermiculation, these ornaments made a general appeal to fantasy and sentiment (48). Wise heads with streaming beards supported an arch over the doorway, in the panel beneath a window satyrs stood watching enviously while a group of nymphs played with Bacchus, throwing grapes around like snowballs. The excesses of Victorian sentiment spawned a family of sickly cherubs, trailing garlands over their naked bodies with a careful modesty. Strictly period ornament this!

Emotional indulgence of this sort is distasteful today but it delighted the Victorians who regarded such things as 'a charming conceit'. Although these subjects are common enough there was also some more acceptable work which was based on mythological subjects. Aesop's Fables were popular and several different sets of designs were made for ceramic tiles by such well known artists as Walter Crane and J. Moyr Smith. A terracotta panel might commemorate a story like George and the Dragon, as in the case of the Passmore Edwards Library in Southwark (49). In this way a building might become a permanent record of some local story or folklore.

The Gothic style encouraged the use of ornamental grotesques and medieval heraldic monsters. In the last quarter of the century these had become part of the general vocabulary of decorative forms and were sold in the catalogues of the decorative art manufacturers. Bizarre serpents, lizards and dragons, made in terracotta, scaled the walls and gables and sat on the roof tops leering at pedestrians (51, 52). Like the naturalistic animals they were there to surprise and amuse people. 'Did you know that there's a dragon sitting on your roof?'' must have been an unwelcome remark from many an aspiring wag. These strange animal forms might also be used with more deliberation. The Imperial Hotel in Russell Square, London (C. F. Doll, 1898, now demolished), had a large Prussian eagle as its emblem (53).

The Victorians lavished particular care and attention on these kind of ornaments. There was something about these monsters that captured the imagination of the sculptor and they invariably showed ingenuity and imagination in the designs. The modelling is lively and detailed, the postures dramatic. While it is possible to question the fitness of such ornament in architecture, these grotesque carvings have a quality that is undeniably attractive. As Ruskin pointed out, they had that combination of beauty and horror that appealed to the Victorians.

Human Scenes and Stories

In many ways this is the most interesting class of ornamental forms, the one in which the Victorians made the greatest contribution to decorative architecture. Statues and the human figure had been used generally in both the Classical and Gothic styles and in the nineteenth century both these precedents were followed. But the Victorians showed considerable originality in what may be called *Illustrated Architecture*. This was pictorial decoration in which large areas of the façade of a building were used to illustrate scenes and stories. The panels were usually made from mosaic or ceramic tiles and some-

48. Cadogan Sq, London SW1; 1886

49/50. Passmore Edwards Library, Southwark, London.
Built in dark plum terracotta
51. Terracotta monster scaling building, St George's,
Bristol 1

times terracotta. Some of these buildings are examined in detail
elsewhere (see chapter 6) and in this section only the general characteristics of the ornamental forms will be discussed.

Ruskin had said that there were particular subjects that were
suitable for the use in illustrating the occupations of man: the instruments of art, agriculture and war (perhaps it is strange that so christian a gentleman should include war), armour and dress, drapery in
general, shipping and architecture itself. These might be described as
the 'noble' occupations of man. Occasionally there are instances
when commerce and technology intrude, where illustrated architecture was used as a form of permanent advertising. But generally
the subjects of these pictures were designed for the moral edification
and education of the people.

Following the Greek idea of telling a story in a frieze, there were
some designs that illustrated a particular event or occupation in a
series of small images. On the sides of the Wedgwood Institute in Stoke-
on-Trent, for instance, the various activities of a potter are depicted
in relief terracotta. In one panel the potter is throwing a pot on a wheel,
in the next the ware is being taken to the kiln for firing, in another
panel artists are shown at work applying the decoration; in sequence
the story unfolds. A similar technique was used in the pictorial decorations for the Albert Hall (55, 56). Like a strip cartoon the images depict
the arts of man, with pictures of astronomers, herbalists, weavers and
painters, architects and builders. The frieze runs around the whole of
the top storey of the circular building beneath the dome, like a wrapper
round a birthday cake. The frieze is composed of maroon and ochre tiles
rather than mosaic and although the lines of the figures appear to be

52. Terracotta dragons on the old Everard Printing
Works, Bristol 1; 1901 (now largely demolished)

53. Detail of Imperial Hotel, Russell Sq (demolished)

54. Coventry Town Hall with painted sculptures

neatly curved they are in fact composed of a vast number of small rectangular sections; the viewing distance is so great that the edges merge into a smooth outline. A year earlier, in 1866, the same technique had been employed in some panels for the central courtyard of the South Kensington Museum (57). In the central pediment a design commemorates the 1851 Exhibition with Queen Victoria receiving tribute from the arts and sciences. Behind her is the outline of Paxton's Crystal Palace.

In each of these examples that have been given the images depict an essential moment of drama in a story or event. The figures are stylised, or rather idealised, in the same way that statues of divinities were. The masons and architects have the same look of a Greek god, the women have that flawless beauty of a Pre-Raphaelite matron. There

55. Royal Albert Hall, London, built in brick and buff terracotta; 1867

56. Detail of frieze

57. Victoria and Albert Museum, London; 1866

is a minimum of detail and clutter in the pictures since they were designed to be viewed from a distance of thirty or forty yards and only clear, bold lines would be seen. As a result this form of ornamentation lacked the fussiness and sentimentality that flawed so much of Victorian decoration. Because this is such a successful decorative form it will be discussed further in the context of individual buildings.

Lettering

This is a form of ornament that was not mentioned by Ruskin but it requires at least a few remarks. Towards the end of the nineteenth century there was considerable interest in typography, largely generated by the efforts of men like William Morris to reassert the true art of printing. It was seen that the letters of the alphabet might be drawn into decorative forms as well as plants or flowers could. Without going into details of the different styles of lettering it should be noted that the characters were made more fluid and ornamental.

The use of lettering in architecture is interesting and while the Victorians used fewer signs and emblems than we do today, they took pains to make their announcements both clear and pleasing. The name of a building might be worked in with an ornamental motif (58), which was often cast in terracotta. Tiles and mosaic were also used, especially in shops. Grocery stores often had their name painted on

65

F

58. Ornamental terracotta panel with lettering, Victoria, London; *c.* 1895

59. Terracotta panel for North London school

glass or moulded in a brass windowsill. Simple but attractive panels were made for the London Board Schools (59).

Written texts were sometimes used in conjunction with pictorial art giving a description of the work, its date and dedication, as in the case of the Albert Hall. Here the lettering forms an integral part of the

60. Blomfield Court, Maida Vale, London W9; *c.* 1895

design and while it can be read clearly, it also acts as a part of the overall ornamentation of the building. Occasionally lettering could form a complete panel of ornament in itself. The illustration at the South Kensington Museum, mentioned in the last section, is flanked by two smaller panels with texts that read:

> Wisdom exalteth her children and layeth hold of them that seek her.
> Wisdom cometh from the Lord and is with Him forever.

To cite one more example of architectural lettering: on the façade of the Everard Building in Bristol (118), there are two complete alphabets. One is that designed by Gutenberg who invented printing, the other is the 'Golden Alphabet' designed by William Morris. Everard was a printer himself and these designs were particularly fit decoration for his new building. Ornamental lettering is a small but significant part of nineteenth-century architectural decoration and one that has particular lessons for contemporary design.

And so it was that decoration, whatever the source, came to be the chief characteristic of the period. The studied historicism of the middle decades of the century developed into a free-for-all in which any style, from any age, was employed for any purpose. This move was assisted by the industrial manufacturers who mass produced architectural ornaments of every kind. This has always brought abuse from those critics who are 'sticklers for an ethical basis to architecture'. Too far outside the canons of good taste, many of the decorative forms of the later nineteenth century have simply been looked upon as vulgar. Eccentric they may be, perhaps ill-judged, always searching for individuality—but although it is rarely noticed they provide some of the most interesting architectural features in our cities today.

5 Materials

There is an interesting relationship between ornamental forms and the building materials that were used during the nineteenth century. It is commonly supposed that one of the follies of Victorian architecture was the inappropriate use of decoration and materials. The argument has largely been put forward by architects this century who felt that building materials should express themselves only in terms of texture, pattern and abstract form. They challenged the integrity with which the Victorians manufactured their architectural enrichments and suggested that their work was false to the real nature of the material. This charge is rarely borne out by the reality of the situation. For the most part, decoration was carefully related to the known potential of the material and its capacity to be worked in the required manner.

Building materials fall into two classes: natural and artificial. Natural materials like stone, wood and slate must always be worked by hand and in the nineteenth century were usually cut and shaped on site. To decorate them was expensive and also difficult since it relied on the availability of skilled labour. Even in the nineteenth century the traditional crafts were dying out (that after all was what William Morris was always complaining about) and so there were not enough men to produce the goods in any quantity. Artificial materials, on the other hand, had to be worked in the factory in any case and some form of mechanical decoration could be integrated easily with the whole manufacturing process.

Mention has been made of the part that Ruskin played in the developing consciousness of what was suitable decoration. He also had some very set ideas on what materials were suitable for building. Just as ornaments should follow nature, so only natural materials were acceptable for true architecture. Because they were man-made, iron and glass could only serve in an auxiliary capacity to assist where they were helpful, like wine 'a man may use it for his infirmity but never for his nourishment'. The Ruskin school of thought had no sympathy with the Functional Tradition. But this rejection of artificial materials was too limiting in the context of city growth. As usual the absolute directives that Ruskin gave (natural forms with natural materials) were modified by practical considerations. The decorative art manufacturers followed some of the forms, but not the materials. None the less, Ruskin's theories were influential and, as we have seen,

61. Music shop, Walsall, with carved stone façade

Victorian architectural ornaments were striving for something of the visual naturalism that he advocated. At the same time the material itself exerted particular constraints on the design process. The result, at best, was not the blind copying of patterns that is often associated with the Victorians, but an interesting combination of technical efficiency and aesthetic theory. This can best be seen by relating the list of ornamental subjects to the materials, both natural and artificial, that were commonly used.

Stone

Stone and marble have always been used in building construction and regional styles developed in accordance with the quality and type of stone available. Just as this is a natural material with which to build, so it has always been used for sculpture and different forms of ornamentation in architecture. In the nineteenth century, however, dressed stone was usually reserved for prestige buildings like churches and town halls, where money and time were not prime considerations. Stone and marble were expensive in every sense and required skilled masons and sculptors. As Ruskin observed, in contradistinction to Morris, it is doubtful whether the average workman had either the skill or inclination to work stone effectively. Thus, where there was an abundance of good local stone, in domestic building it was used for the main structure while the ornaments were often factory made or bought from a stone mason by the yard. Many examples can be found in a city like Bristol—a group of houses in Manilla Road, Clifton, for instance, display a rather unhappy combination of stone walls and terracotta details for the window frames. Alternatively, the decorative part of the design was supplied in other materials such as stained-glass, fretted barge-boards or ornamental metalwork.

There are a number of commercial buildings that have carved stone façades, although terracotta was more commonly used and stonework was reserved for occasions where there was little or no repetition in the parts of the design. Such work was specially commissioned, as in the case of H. Taylor's music shop in Walsall (61) which is illustrated with musical instruments, busts of famous musicians and small panels depicting bands of minstrels. However, the building rather demonstrates the shortcomings of stone when compared with similar work in a different material (*vide* the Everard Building, Bristol: (116 p. 112ff.). The building is desperately in need of a thorough clean for a start (stone has a fatal fascination for soot) and the detail of the carving is so small as to be almost lost when viewed from street level, though this is perhaps more the fault of the designer than of the material. Townsend's Horniman Museum gives a better impression of what could be achieved with ornamental stonework (93). The building has been discussed often enough, but it is still worth praising the beautifully sculpted form of the clock tower with the Art Nouveau floral motifs that cling to the strangely helmeted corner turrets. Here the stone has been shaped with the freedom of clay, while the rest of the building maintains the rectilinear quality of stone blocks, which is a happy combination of freedom and control that expresses the nature of the material.

62. Flint and terracotta church, Muswell Hill, North
London; 1902

Stonework becomes most significant when used for public buildings.
This an area of architecture that has not been given a great deal of
attention since this book is primarily concerned with manufactured
ornament. But it is important to consider the influence of prestige
buildings on the lower categories of architectural expression. Ornamental forms that were used for the new palace of Westminster (Sir
Charles Barry and Pugin 1840–52) or the new Foreign Offices in Whitehall (G. G. Scott designed 1861) were used as examples by many other
architects who were not working on such a grand scale but reflected
the changing fashions and styles of the period. Whether Gothic or
Classical in their derivation these elaborate 'competition' designs
provided the inspiration for a host of lesser buildings. But the statues,
gargoyles, moulded panels and encrusted pinnacles which were carved
in stone in one case were cast (much more cheaply) in terracotta in
another.

In the later decades of the century, artificial materials became
increasingly popular and lost some of the opprobrium of being a poor

relation to stone. It is interesting that Gilbert Scott's Martyr's Memorial in Oxford (1841) was made entirely of stone while his later design for the Albert Memorial (1863–72) made extensive use of artificial materials for decoration. And yet stone has always been regarded as the most luxurious of building materials—even today developers delight in lining the entrance of a new building with panels of veined marble to give it an assumed elegance, a bit of class, and in this way making it more rentable.

Flint

Flint has always been used to obtain a decorative surface, either in combination with stone or brick. Flint and brick walls are commonly found in the chalk districts of Britain. Because of their small, irregular shape, flints can rarely be used where they take the full thrust of the building load; instead they are formed into regular patterns or panels of surface decoration. In Muswell Hill, London, there is an interesting example of the use of this material in the United Reformed Church, Muswell Hill Broadway (62). Here the main structural lines of the building are in dark red terracotta, while the infil panels are faced with flint. Built in 1902 the building achieves that jewel-like quality that was popular at the time. The flints have a natural 'glazed' surface that is almost ceramic and this is a subtle compliment to the matt finish of the terracotta. Whilst flint was not widely used in combination with artificial materials this building demonstrates the happy effects that could be achieved.

63. Slates forming geometric patterns, East Finchley,
London

64. Half-timbered buildings recently repainted, Bristol Centre

66. Carved wooden door panels, Shaftesbury Avenue, London

65. Clifton Court, Maida Vale, London

67. Barge-boards and terracotta dragon, detail Imperial
Hotel, Henley-on-Thames

Slate

One of the least attractive elements in modern architecture has been
the flat roof. Looking at a building strictly in visual terms, the pitch
roof can provide the most lovely surface of the structure. The particular contribution of the Victorians in this case was to extend the
traditional vocabulary of the various rectangular shaped slates to
include a variety of other geometrical shapes that formed linear patterns (63). They also introduced different colours. Ruskin had set a
precedent for this with the purple and green slates that were used for
the Oxford Debating Rooms (Deane and Woodward 1857). With their
love of small gables and turrets the Victorians found plenty of opportunities to explore the possibilities for new decorative effects.

Wood

Elizabethan-style half-timbering, with its connotation of burgher respectability, was a popular form of decorative architecture in the late
nineteenth century. The black and white façades are familiar enough
and require little comment, except to point out the variety of effects
that could be achieved through different patterns of construction.
Timber was not used just for its ornamental quality but as an integral
part of a reproduction style of building (64, 65).

Wood carving was necessarily confined to small detail work in
windows and doorways. Panelled doors often received quite elaborate

treatment, especially in mansion blocks and other buildings with large entrances. The outer doors, which were closed at night, might be decorated with swags of fruit and sometimes the name of the building. Exeter Mansions in Shaftesbury Avenue, London, is a typical example (66).

Another way in which wood was put to decorative use can be seen on the gable-end of almost every Victorian house where barge-boards formed an ornamental screen as a finishing detail to the roof (67). An almost endless variety of designs can be found, some fretted, some pierced, some with applied strip patterns; each one differs according to the pitch of the roof and the length and depth of the board. At the time when the Queen Anne style was popular, wood was also used for balcony railings. They were usually painted white, forming a bright contrast with the red brick. Another ornamental use of woodwork that is worth remembering is the chevron fascias that were once so characteristic of British railway stations.

Finally some mention must be made of the use of wood in the Victorian cottage style that is known as *cottage-orné*. Branches, stripped of twigs, were used to make decorative porches and frames. It was an attempt to capture a picturesque rural flavour which was inspired by the mood of 'back to nature for the week-end'. The idea might have a certain charm if sufficient honeysuckle was growing over the porch!

Brick

In its basic form the Victorians used brick in a customary way, paying attention to the visual effects of different bonds and joints. They also borrowed regional styles in combining brick with other materials often using concrete and terracotta instead of flint or stone. Following the lead of William Butterfield's 'constructional polychromy' decorative effects were often achieved by the combination of different coloured bricks. Butterfield's technique was exemplified in his designs for Keble College, Oxford (1868) and Rugby School (1872). The banding of different coloured bricks was supposed to suggest the internal structure of the building and whilst it is not always successful this form of decoration could provide some light relief from the grey monotony of sooty bricks. In suburban terrace houses, white brick outlines and string courses with red brick infill was a common combination (68).

None of which is very startling. But with little extra effort the surface of the brick could be shaped during the manufacturing process. This was done in two ways. In the second half of the century many bricks were pressed by machine using dry powdered clay. It was easy to place a die at the bottom of the mould, which formed a pattern on the face of the brick. The design had to be simple because the clay was coarse and would not take a delicate impression. So bold low-relief floral and geometric patterns were used (69, 70), each one forming a complete image to avoid confusion for the bricklayers (who even then were notoriously careless). Bricks were also made from wet or plastic clay and moulded by hand. The clay was pressed into plaster of paris formers which had been cast from an original prepared by a sculptor. The plaster absorbed some of the moisture from the clay which, when it

68. Red and white brick terrace, Henley-on-Thames

69. Dust-pressed brick inserts with low relief design

RAYMOND'S PERFECTION PRESS.

70. Press for making ornamental bricks; 1886 patent

had sufficiently contracted, was lifted from the mould and taken away to be fired. The mould itself was undamaged and could be re-used. This second process allowed for more subtle patterns and carved subjects in higher relief (72). Swags of fruit, fauns, satyrs and mythical beasts were common and in the seventies and eighties panels of sunflowers, lilies and pomegranates were popular expressions of the Aesthetic Movement.

As far as the manufacturing process is concerned there is nothing false about using brick in this way. Clay is a sculptural material and so the Victorians were, in many ways, being more truthful to the medium rather than falsifying it. It is only possible to conclude that the rejection of decorative brickwork is based on economic rather than theoretical or purist principles.

71. Decorative panel in sculpted brick,
Mayfair London; *c.* 1895

72. Sculptured brick panel, Thos Goode's, Mayfair;
1876

Terracotta

Terracotta was worked in a similar manner to bricks made from
plastic clay, though the composition of the material was different and
the decorative possibilities far greater. Terracotta was usually fairly
massive and blocks 12 to 15 inches deep and three or four feet square
were commonly used (73). To reduce the weight the sections were
hollow, although this did not impair their structural properties.
Terracotta was effectively an artificial stone but with few of the

73. Constructional block of terracotta, as from 52

74. Buff terracotta panel, school, Worcester; *c.* 1890

disadvantages of the natural material. It could be formed to almost any shape (undercutting in the design was done after it was taken from the mould), produced in a wide range of colours (with the addition of chemical dyes) and any one shape could be accurately reproduced as often as required from the same plaster mould. Properly made it was more resistant to weathering than stone and since it was made at the pottery it was not subject to any of the difficulties of working on site. Best of all, perhaps, terracotta sculpture could be moulded by any practised labourer. Thus the problem of finding skilled masons did not arise.

As a decorative medium it is fair to say that terracotta excelled all others. Examples can be found that cover each of Ruskin's categories of decoration and it is difficult to nominate any one kind of treatment that was more suited to the material than another; wherever stone could be used for a building, so too could terracotta (74–6, 78). The Victorians loved terracotta and there were few architects who did not use it. Alfred Waterhouse is considered to have been responsible for its general acceptance and popularity—Manchester Town Hall (1868–77), Balliol College, Oxford (1867) and the Natural History Museum, London (1881) are typical of his work. The value of terracotta is here summed up by C. T. Davis, an American writing at the end of the century:

Terracotta is today the most available material used for the construction of

75. Terracotta as stone, Cardinal Vaughan College,
Addison Rd, London W11

76. Stourbridge Library, by F. Woodward; 1904

77. Detail of door panel, Stourbridge Library

buildings of all classes and forms. It is, in fact, the concrete part of them. It is, as well, indispensable in every assemblage of artistic architectural ornamentation and has virtually taken the place of stone and is now used in the completion of seven-tenths of the structures erected. . . . In beauty of colour it has an advantage over stone, for by the use of chemicals almost any colour can be produced, and they are found to be less apt to change under atmospheric influences. In terracotta we can find a scope for freedom, with a capacity for supplying the increasing demand for decoration in the most durable material.*

The Victorian use of terracotta must be seen in this context of the 'increasing demand for decoration'. The material was adaptable to

* Davis C. T. *A Practical Treatise on the Manufacture of Bricks, Tiles and Terracotta*, 1895; pp. 468–9.

78. Constructional terracotta, South Audley St, Mayfair, London; *c.* 1895

79. Brick and terracotta, Gloucester, *c.* 1900

80. Terracotta monsters and window detail, London W8

almost any demand that the designer could make, whether for small pieces of ornament like the dragons and vaguely mythical beasts that scaled the walls of brick buildings (80) or for a thorough-going system of construction that had the decorative scheme built into it, such as the buildings in Mount Street, Mayfair (81, 82, 83). And yet it is wrong to assume that terracotta had to have some form of surface decoration, as Waterhouse's Natural History Museum demonstrates it was possible to obtain very satisfactory results by just using a plain surface and the colour of the material. Although the Victorians were not contradicting the nature of the material by developing its sculptural quality, the close association between terracotta and the Decorative Tradition has belied its real functional value as a building material.

85

81. Terracotta buildings, Mount St, Mayfair; 1893   82/83. Details of 81

Tiles

Tile making was one of the great art industries of the period. With their inclination to historicism, the Victorian critics were keen to point out that tiles had been used in architectural decoration for almost as long as man had been building. The nineteenth-century tile industry was exceptional in that mass-production techniques were introduced—for floor tiles (encaustic) after Samuel Wright's patent of 1830, and for wall tiles after Prosser's dust press patent of 1840. In company with terracotta, ceramic tiles provided the ideal material of the Decorative Tradition:

The efforts of many generations to discover an absolutely imperishable medium which they could use in their work have probably produced nothing which fulfils this essential condition better than glazed earthenware. This manufactured material by the hardness of surface, its capacity for receiving almost any kind of colour from the most delicate tints to the deepest and richest hues and the ease by which it can be adapted to very diverse purposes, is peculiarly fitted for architectural ornament.*

There are three categories of tiles that must be distinguished. *Floor* tiles, whether figured encaustic or the smaller geometric sections, were used inside and out for hallways, paths and verandas. Geometric pavements were common in suburban houses (84). Encaustic tiles with heraldic, floral and abstract motifs were usually reserved for churches and civic buildings. *Wall* tiles, mostly seen in porches (85, 86) employed

* Baldry, A Lys, *Modern Mural Decoration*, 1902; p. 110.

84. Suburban doorway with geometric pavement, South London

85/86. Panels of wall tiles in porches, London and Cardiff

87. Yellow-brown architectural faience, Madox St,
London W1; 1892

LADIES ROOM

88. Tilework on platform, Shrub Hill station, Worcester

89. Pub with architectural faience, Belfast c. 1895

any number of decorative styles, using either a transfer-printed pattern or brightly coloured glazes over an embossed design. The third category, *architectural faience*, was used for ornamental façades, shopfronts and any kind of external glazed decoration (87, 118). The pieces were cast from plastic clay, using plaster of paris moulds (as with terracotta) and then coloured with various glazes. The decoration was either pictorial, on flat surfaces, or sculpted in low relief. In the latter case there were two basic differences between tiles and terracotta— tiles received a high temperature firing and so the pieces had to be smaller and less delicately carved and while terracotta was unglazed, with a coloured body, tiles could be glazed with a variety of permanent colours.

There are still a good many tiled buildings to be seen in Britain. Because they were glazed tiles provided a bright, clean surface that was popular for food shops and public houses (89, 115). The full possibili-

90. Green and yellow tiles with terracotta, Terminus
Terrace, Southampton; 1907

ties of the medium were rarely exploited for architectural purposes
and the best tilework is often found inside rather than outside a building. But Everard's and the Michelin building (see chapter 6) indicate
the potential that was there. Smaller schemes like the tiled façade of a
building in Percy Street, London (92) show the brightness and fresh
simplicity that even a modest design could provide.*

Mosaic

Mosaic was like beer, so William Morris is supposed to have remarked—
a little of it was no good! The qualities of the medium are best shown
in some of Townsend's buildings: the Horniman Museum which had a
large façade panel designed by R. Anning Bell (94) and the Whitechapel
Art Gallery, London, with a Walter Crane design. Townsend's attitude
to mosaic decoration is typical of a more general outlook. He had a
'strongly felt wish to enlist the aid of design and colour, and, above all,
thought, to render London's façades less monotonously grey and
more full of thought and interest'.† These words would make a suitable epitaph for the architects of the late nineteenth century.

Mosaic was made from small sections cut from glazed ceramic tiles.
The pieces were glued down on to a full-size layout of the design,
following the lines and colours of the drawing. Cement was then spread
over the back of the panel between the pieces of mosaic, to fix them

* For more detailed information on tiles, see Barnard, Julian *Victorian Ceramic Tiles*,
Studio Vista, London; 1972.
† Townsend, in RIBA *Journal*, 3rd series, 1901; Vol. viii, No. 10; pp. 221–41.

91. Decorative metal, granite, glass and tiles, Deptford
High St, London; *c.* 1890

92. Glazed brick building, Percy St, London W1; *c.* 1900

together. When the mosaic was set in position the paper could be stripped away to reveal the design.

Mosaic was largely a pictorial medium, worked to specially prepared designs. These were often linked to some form of symbolic expression of the function of the building, such as those for Scott's Emulsion, Southall (126, 127) and Westminster Cathedral (95). Mosaic, like ceramic tiles, was an ideal vehicle for permanent advertising. For wall panels bold images were essential and like stained-glass the figures benefited from a black outline and dramatic contrasts both in colour and design. Floor mosaic, which was more common, needed more detail because of the viewing range. Many of the tile manufacturers made mosaic and supplied standard designs as well as special commissions. The names of shops were often set in mosaic; since the medium was worked entirely by hand many small one-off designs were executed.

93. Horniman Museum, London SE23; 1901

94. Detail of plate 93—large mosaic by R. Anning Bell

95. Mosaic West portal, Westminster Cathedral, *c.* 1903

Concrete

Concrete was not generally used for ornamental work since the wooden shuttering used in casting allowed for no undercutting in the design. Thus while some details found in terrace houses, such as Montrose Villas (27, 28) may have the appearance of painted concrete, only the columns would in fact be made from this material while the decorative capitals and plaques were terracotta. Nonetheless, concrete was used for lintels and frames, often with a small repeating egg and dart-type pattern and so it played a part in the overall scheme of decoration.

Metal

There were three stages in the casting of metal: the making of the pattern, the moulding and the founding. Moulding controlled the pattern to a large extent; for cheap work only a two part mould could be used and so bi-lateral symmetry was preferable and there could be no undercutting in the design. Simple cast iron railings were therefore the most immediately suitable work (96). But metal casting was a skillful trade and the most elaborate work was possible, the controlling principle being that the more complex the design was the more moulds required and so the more expensive the article became. Decorative cast-ironwork was rarely made to a commissioned design but was bought from manufacturers' catalogues (98, 99).

Wrought iron differs chemically from cast iron in the carbon content.

96. Simple cast iron railing, Clifton, Bristol

97. Window balconies enliven these terrace houses at Whitby, Yorkshire

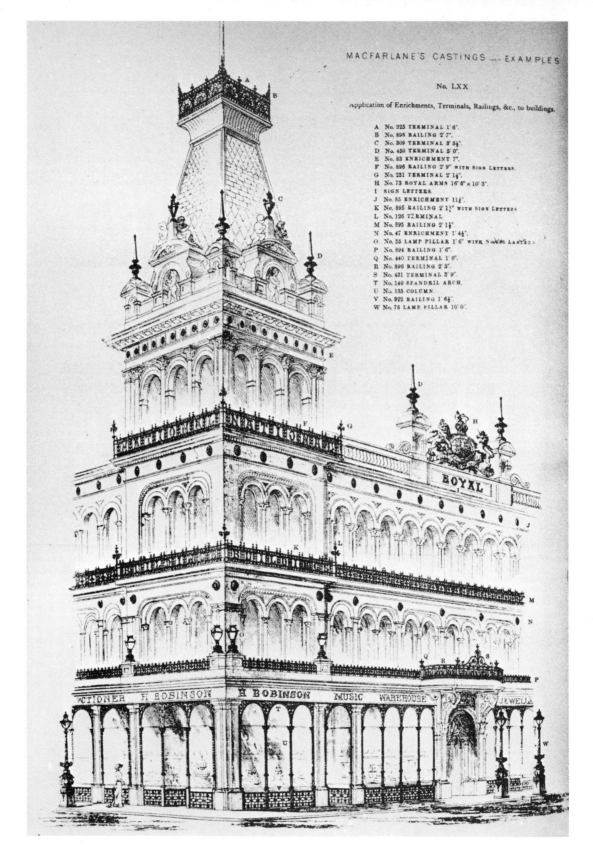

No. LXX

Application of Enrichments, Terminals, Railings, &c., to buildings.

A No. 325 TERMINAL 1' 6".
B No. 898 RAILING 2' 7".
C No. 309 TERMINAL 3' 3½".
D No. 450 TERMINAL 5' 0".
E No. 83 ENRICHMENT 7".
F No. 896 RAILING 2' 9" WITH SIGN LETTERS.
G No. 231 TERMINAL 2' 1½".
H No. 73 ROYAL ARMS 16' 6" × 10' 3".
I SIGN LETTERS.
J No. 85 ENRICHMENT 11½".
K No. 895 RAILING 2' 1½" WITH SIGN LETTERS.
L No. 126 TERMINAL.
M No. 895 RAILING 2' 1½".
N No. 47 ENRICHMENT 1' 4½".
O No. 35 LAMP PILLAR 1' 6" WITH LANTERN.
P No. 894 RAILING 1' 6".
Q No. 440 TERMINAL 1' 0".
R No. 896 RAILING 2' 3".
S No. 431 TERMINAL 3' 9".
T No. 140 SPANDRIL ARCH.
U No. 135 COLUMN.
V No. 922 RAILING 1' 6½".
W No. 76 LAMP PILLAR 10' 0".

98. MacFarlane's castings, enrichments, terminals and balcony railings

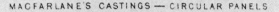
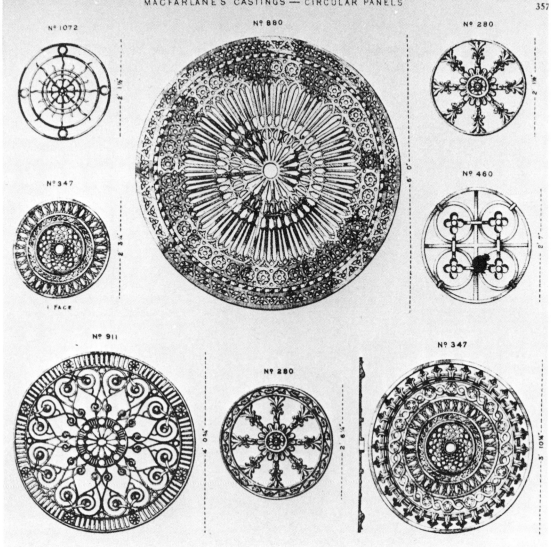

99. Mandala-like circular castings, MacFarlane's

But for the purposes of ornament the important distinction is that wrought iron is malleable and so can be worked to shape by hand. Iron comes to life in its wrought condition and the most delicate forms were made (101, 102) and in the Art Nouveau period fantastic designs were produced that clearly show the capabilities of the material.

The Victorian use of metal requires a study in itself. It must be admitted that it was often applied rather casually as a decorative material. As in Georgian architecture it was employed as superficial decoration for railings, balustrades and architectural vignettes. The style of the decoration is more complex in the later nineteenth century but the application is the same. It could be argued that the engineers were the only people who used iron to proper effect in an architectural sense. Decoration was usually integrated with the structure, filling the open spandrels of an arch in a way that rarely upsets the simplicity of the form (104, 105).

100. Cast iron fountain with typically florid ornaments,
Merthyr Tydfil

101. Wrought iron railings, Gower St, London WC1   102. Detail

104. Smithfield Market, 1868

103. Town clock, Stourbridge, cast locally; 1857

Glass

The importance of glass as a decorative medium can eventually be traced to the revival of interest in Gothic architecture, although the use of coloured glass in the suburban front doors of the 1900s is a far cry from Chartres and Sainte Chapelle. But the Gothic masterpieces inspired the Victorian church-builders, who inspired the secular architects, who were imitated by other architects, who were copied by the manufacturers who supplied the glass ... a route that typifies the progression (or digression) of many decorative materials to popular taste.

There were basically two kinds of architectural decorative glasswork in the nineteenth century. Both had their imitations in the popular market. *Mosaic* glass, which used small pieces of coloured glass with leaded divisions to make up the image, was the traditional stained-glass of medieval ancestry. The picture was bold and rarely figurative, though superficial shading was sometimes used in the nineteenth century to obtain a realistic representation. *Enamelled*

105. Archway, North London; 1897

glass was painted with colours and worked in such a way that the separate pieces were disguised; the result was intended to look rather like a translucent oil painting. A simplified form of mosaic glass was used in suburban front door panels (107, 108). Enamelled glass was imitated for the popular market with the help of transfer printing (109). The visual distinction between the two was the emphasis on colour in one case and the image or pattern in the other.

Coloured glass became very popular in domestic architecture around the turn of the century, in doors, windows and even as panels in the porch (110). It became fashionable as a form of decoration among the lower class of householders to the extent that some enterprising printer even made multicoloured sheets of paper that could be stuck to the inside of the window to give the impression of stained glass!

Stucco
Among the categories of materials listed here, ornamental plaster-work deserves a special mention, although it was not manufactured in the sense that terracotta and tiles were. Up until about 1860 stucco was applied almost universally as a plain external render over bricks; by the turn of the century it became popular again as a rough cast 'pebble dash' in imitation of C. F. A. Voysey's work. But it was not used

Domestic Glass for H.W. MEADE-KING Esq. West Derby Liverpool.

Drawing Room.

Drawing Room.

Cate Room Window.

Bed Room.

Copyright Entered at Stationers Hall.

Shrigley & Hunt Lancaster & London.

106. Catalogue of domestic glass, Shrigley & Hunt; 1879

107/108. Coloured glass in terrace houses, London NW3; c. 1900

109. Transfer-printed glass

generally for external decoration, although in a debased form the traditional 'pargetting' technique can sometimes be found. A repeating pattern was sometimes pressed into the facial render or window lintel. Rather clumsy patterns were also carved by hand in the wet plaster which was then painted around the design (usually a floral pattern) giving a colourful, if not very sophisticated form of surface decoration (111). Pargetting was a traditional craft in East Anglia but Victorian examples can be found in several places in southern England. A large half-timbered building in the market square in Salisbury has this kind of decoration, for instance. A form of mural painting that was particularly successful can be seen on the walls of an old dairy building on Crouch Hill in north London (122, 123 p. 115ff.). The design was painted on to wet render using specially prepared colours—it was an external

110. Printed and coloured glass porch panel, Barkston Gardens, London SW5

111. Unsophisticated designs carved into wet plaster, East Finchley, London

112/113. Ornamental plasterwork, recently repainted, Henley-on-Thames; *c.* 1895

form of *fresco* painting.

This list may not be comprehensive but it does indicate the general way in which the Victorians made use of the materials available to produce decorative schemes. Perhaps the most important point to bring out is that different materials were used according to the 'level' of architecture in a hierarchy that ran from church building down to suburban housing. Different materials were used and yet they expressed the same superficial forms of decoration. If it was possible to achieve a similar visual effect by using different materials and more efficient means of production, then that was a satisfactory expedient to satisfy the demands of the majority of the population who otherwise would be deprived of ornamental architecture.

6 City Buildings
in the Decorative Tradition

By the end of the nineteenth century, the Decorative Tradition was as well established in the mind of the public as the International Style was the 1950s. Materials were available that could be moulded to any style, worked into any form. With the assistance of machinery, architectural ornaments were being mass produced and made available to everyone. The architect was an artist, alive with ideas and possibilities. Gone forever, or so it seemed, was the drab uniformity of Georgian London. The streets were singing with colour and variety, or if they were not there was no possible reason to prevent them being so. In a presidential address to the *National Association for the Advancement of Art and its Application to Industry*, Lord Leighton was able to speak with some satisfaction of the increasing consciousness of the importance of art and decoration in the city landscape:

Are not statues multiplying in our streets? Is not architecture, as an art, finding at this time, increasing if tardy acceptance at the hands of private individuals? Is not a wholesome sense dawning among us that even a private dwelling should not offend, nay, should conciliate the eye of the passer-by in our public thoroughfares? ... I acknowledge with joy that there is ... much on which we may justly congratulate ourselves, much that points to a quickening consciousness, a stirring of the aesthetic impulse.*

Of course it is easy to romanticise the image of Victorian urban life; however attractive the architecture might be it was no good if you could not see it under all the grime and soot. There was no clean air act and by all accounts the city was a filthy place. But this only furnished another reason for designing colourful and decorative buildings. Stone and brick were soon disfigured by atmospheric pollution and were badly stained within a very short time. Only in recent years have we begun to discover some of the treasures that lie hidden under the layers of dirt. That is why the Victorians were so keen on terracotta and glazed tiles. These materials were pretty well impervious and every storm of rain acted as a detergent washing the building clean, rather than forcing the dirt further into the absorbent fabric. Glazed tiles, in particular, can be seen to have retained the brightness of their original colours over a period of seventy or eighty years.

* *National Association for the Advancement of Art and its Application to Industry*, 1888; p. 16.

114. Debenham's old house, Addison Rd, London W11; 1906

Colour is probably the most neglected element in English architecture. For some reason we have always fought shy of using it to any great extent. In other countries the buildings are alive with colour. But English reserve and supposedly the English climate, has so often stultified our imagination. We are inhibited by the control of rational theories of design. We go abroad and marvel at the arab mosque, at the murals of moorish tiles, but that is a holiday and 'good taste' prevents our thinking in similar terms about our own architecture when we return. Architecture, more especially decorative architecture, should make us happy. As Ruskin observed, that is the purpose of all ornament, to make us happy. But there is a strong puritanical streak in the architecture of England and it is particularly evident in the products of the Modern Movement. Somehow we have got it into our heads that our architecture must never be happy or amusing. If we suggest that our buildings are boring and unattractive we are quickly silenced with the reply that it is the public's ignorance and lack of taste that fails to appreciate the subtle qualities of proportion and form. We have leanred to live passively with an architectural environment from which we derive no pleasure.

Substantially the same arguments were employed at the end of the nineteenth century by Halsey Ricardo, an architect who was dedicated to the use of colour in building. We are so grateful for any small attention that is shown us in the street, he said, we see a basket of flowers and we are immediately delighted. Why cannot we be delighted in the same way by the buildings that surround us?

It so happens that I am frequently in sight of a wall built by Mr De Morgan and faced with his tiles. I have seen it at all seasons, under all weathers, in all lights and twilights, and it is always a feast and a rest to the eyes. Think of whole streets vibrating with harmonies of colour . . .. It is within our reach and moreover it is profoundly sensible.*

Ricardo and other contemporary critics always referred to Italian precedents, extolling the virtues of the picturesque buildings in Venice and Florence. English architecture, they said, was too correct and unimaginative, drab and boring:

The result of this stony scholarship of our streets is that we can't live in them. Every evening thousands escape by every railway from the masterpieces of correct architecture . . . to the shelter of the country where the earth is green about them and the heaven blue above them. Cannot we make our streets a little more kindly and comforting to those poor prisoners who cannot escape? We have tried mass and form, and light and shade; might we not now have an attempt at colour?†

Ricardo's theories on colour and design were made manifest in a house that he built in Addison Road, near Holland Park in London (114). The building, completed in 1907, was commissioned by Sir Ernest Debenham, of Debenham and Freebody's the Oxford Street store. The outside of the house is entirely clad in glazed ceramics. The main structural features are in white *Carrara Ware* faience, made by Doulton's of Lambeth. Each of the wide arches on the façade frames a window on the ground and first floor, with panels of green glazed bricks in between. At the second floor level there is a string course of shaped tiles which casts a regular shadow on to the flat spandrels of the arches, each of which has a circular disc of decoration on the centre line of the column. The second story has a balcony which runs the length of the front of the building with white columns supporting the eaves. The wall behind is covered with glazed bricks in various shades of blue, which form geometric patterns on either side of the windows. Both the green and the blue glazed bricks were manufactured by the Leeds Fireclay Company. The roofing tiles, which are shaped like the traditional mediterranean *tuile canale,* are a darker green than the wall tiles but in a matching tone and were imported from Spain.

* Halsey Ricardo in RIBA *Journal*, 3rd Series, Vol. III, 1896; p. 365ff.
† Halsey Ricardo, paper to the Society of Arts in *Journal of the Society of Arts*; 1902.

A covered pathway leads up to the front of the house, one side of which is open with piers in blue-grey semi-vitrified Staffordshire bricks. On the inside of the facing wall are some of the famous De Morgan tiles with predominantly blue designs in the style of Persian ceramics. At the end of the arcade, next to the door, is a small tile mural with a stylised Tuscan landscape and information about the architect and the date of the building. Inside the house are many more De Morgan tiles and in the main hall a magnificent mosaic mural designed by Walter Crane. The interior decoration does not concern us here, unfortunately. But as one might expect, while bold areas of plain colours are used externally, the internal decorations are delicate and elaborate; the two are linked by the covered entrance which connects the internal-external spaces with a corresponding complexity of decoration.

De Morgan's pottery closed down in 1907 and for this house Ricardo used the best of the tiles in stock. The two men had earlier been in partnership together and clearly the work at Addison Road was as much the responsibility of the potter as it was of the architect. Ricardo and De Morgan shared similar views on colour and decoration and but for De Morgan's ill health one might have expected more work in a similar vein. De Morgan, too, used to dream of streets alive with colour and in a paper delivered to the *Society of Arts*, in 1892, on the history of lustre he pointed out that 'one obvious use of lustreware is its application to domes and towers and to all parts of buildings that catch the level rays of the sun'. Here was a Blakean vision of the golden city!

Ceramic tiles were used extensively during the later decades of the nineteenth century. They are most commonly found as small panels of decoration lining the porches of suburban houses, although complete façades of polychrome ceramic tiles were also made. As Baldry said, tiles provided the most effective surface for permanent decoration. Of course a lot of such buildings have been lost through changes in popular taste and in the two spates of wilful destruction that have been witnessed this century: the bombing during the Second World War and the more recent demolition brought about by comprehensive redevelopment and modern property speculators. Yet there are still a few examples and they show the quality and value of the material and the considerable freedom that it offered for decorative design.

Most of the early chain-stores like Lipton's, David Greig's and Sainsbury's used tiles in their shops, partly because the material was hygienic and also because it provided a form of house-styling in the repetition of certain designs—a lot of the David Greig shops, for instance, used tiles with a thistle motif. The shop fronts are usually tiled as well, with the company name either painted on glass or cast as a panel of tiles. Chard's in Gloucester Road, West London, is a fine example in brown, buff and blue faience with moulded ornaments in a confusion of styles that is typical of late Victorian design (115). Inside butcher's shops especially there are often murals with drawings of pigs, cattle or poultry. The most elaborate scheme of this sort can be seen in the Meat Halls of Harrods', Knightsbridge, where a series of cartoons with hunting scenes decorate the walls. It is sad to see so many of these old shops being modernised; although it is easy to under-

115. Architectural faience, Gloucester Rd, London SW7; *c.* 1895

stand the practical necessity of enlarging and reorganising the premises, all the charm and humour is lost and all that is left is just another clinical supermarket. The rationale of modern design makes another killing.

It has been stressed that an essential aspect of the Decorative Tradition is individuality. So often it is difficult to know what exactly goes on inside a building. An anonymous façade might shield a restaurant, an office, even an information bureau. It is not until you peer around and find the small type that you can read who uses the building.

Alternatively in the case of those who want to broadcast their presence, neon signs disfigure the street with a crude aggression that blunts our awareness. Both architecture and advertising are so lacking in sensitivity. But here is a contrast—look at the Edward Everard Printing Works in Broad Street, Bristol (116, 117, 118), or the old dairy building at the bottom of Crouch Hill, London N4 (121, 122, 123). Both are perfect examples of what has been called *illustrated architecture*, where the decoration so eloquently describes the function of the building.

The Everard Building was completed in 1902. Although the site of the printing works has recently been redeveloped, parts of the old building have been preserved and neatly married into the new scheme. The façade is composed of tiles made by Doulton's of Lambeth and the illustrations were designed by W. J. Neatby, who was in charge of the company's architectural department. Simply in terms of style the building is interesting since it is one of the few architectural examples of English Art Nouveau. But its significance is more than historical. It embodies all the best attributes of the Decorative Tradition.

116. The old Everard Printing Works, Bristol; 1902

117. Everard's, detail; allegorical figure representing
Light and Truth

118. Gutenberg, Morris and the Spirit of Literature,
symbolising the craft revival in printing

Everard was a printer and so he wanted his new building to be a monument to the craft of printing. To symbolise this there are pictures of Gutenberg, who is seen at work at his fifteenth-century printing press, and opposite him, William Morris, who was instrumental in re-establishing the art of the printer which had been debased by commercial interests during the nineteenth century. Between the two men, who are flanked by the alphabets that they designed, is the *Spirit of Literature* which symbolically links them together. At the top of the building is another allegorical figure holding a lamp and a mirror—the literary symbols of Light and Truth. Beneath the two arched windows on the first floor is the name of the printing house in an Art Nouveau typeface which was designed by Everard for the purpose. All the images were painted directly on to the tiles using ceramic colours that were fired and later sealed beneath a clear glaze; they are permanent and unaffected by any kind of weathering.

In an immediate sense the façade is a giant advertisement and it clearly states the function of the building. But with what grace and kindness that message is conveyed. It is also a monument, a permanent memorial to printing. For as Everard was anxious to point out,* it seemed a pity that famous men should only be commemorated in statues, paintings and books—why not in architecture too? The building is also a sort of gift to the people of Bristol—it is not insignificant that when the building was completed and the drapes removed, so many people came to see it that the police had to regulate the traffic in Broad Street for several days. What a thought! Crowds of people who actually wanted to look at a new building. Such a thing is unheard of today. The public shows no interest in modern architecture because modern architecture provides nothing to be interested in.

The Michelin Building in Fulham Road, London (119, 120) is similar to Everard's though not so successful in many ways. It was designed in 1909 by two Frenchmen, François Espinasse (arch.) and Gilardoni (tilework). The insignia of the firm and the name, Michelin Tyre Co. are used as decoration in many places, but the real interest was to be found in the tiled panels that illustrated contemporary racing cars, forming a gallery of fame for the early enthusiasts. In this

* See Everard's own book: *A Bristol Printing House*, 1902.

119. Michelin Building, Fulham Rd, London; 1909

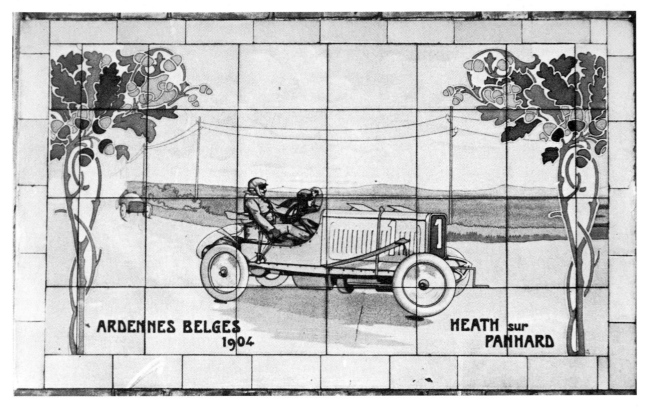

120. Detail of plate 119

way architecture could provide interest and information for the public, just as the Bristol building did. This was an aspect of architecture that Walter Crane wished to promote. As he said:

The decoration of public buildings should be the highest form of popular art, as it was in the Middle Ages, when a town-hall, or church, was no bad equivalent for a public library stored with legends and symbols—histories as they were, which impressed themselves upon the unlettered, through the vivid language of design.*

Few buildings received quite such dramatic treatment as the Everard building, but there are several others that show the same approach. The old dairy at Crouch Hill (121, 122, 123) was mentioned earlier and it is certainly a good example of illustrated architecture. Again the decoration acts as an advertisement, but one is hardly aware of the commercial interest. The pictures of grazing cows, milking, cooling, making butter and milk delivery are instructive and evocative. They are of great curiosity value now since they are historical records, but a hundred years ago they were, as Walter Crane advocated, a lively text book for those who knew nothing of country life and the ways of dairy farming. In the country one would see real cows, but then, as now, many people never had the opportunity to get out of the city. It is true that people could be educated with books, but what book could provide illustrations like these, even if you were able to read? Surely this is

* Crane, Walter, 'Of the Decoration of Public Buildings', in *Art and Life and the Building and Decoration of Cities*, a series of lectures by members of the Arts and Crafts Exhibition Society, 1896; p. 138.

121. Old dairy buildings, Crouch Hill, London N4; *c.* 1875

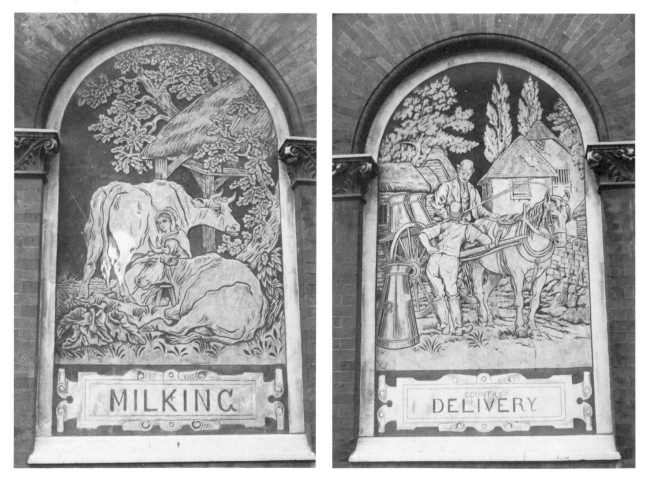

122. Detail of plate 121; a vivid illustration in red and white fresco

123. Detail of 121

124. Royal College of Organists, Kensington Gore, London

125. Detail of plate 124, designs by F. Moody, 1883

126. Scott's Emulsion, Southall, Middlesex; 1906

the most perfect and natural form of architecture, giving interest, colour and variety to the streets of the city.

There are similar pictures on the walls of the Royal College of Organists in Kensington (124, 125). The building is well known, though if comparisons were to made it could hardly be said that the illustrations are as graphic as the ones just mentioned, which hardly anyone has heard of. It is sad how many good things get neglected. But the Royal College of Organists is a fun building and next to the monolithic greyness of the Royal College of Art it is a positive joy. All the defensive arguments against using colour in English architecture are refuted again in this building—it is not badly affected by the climate and the strong contrasts of red and white sings out in all weathers. With the Albert Hall and the Albert Memorial nearby this part of London has a small concentration of illustrated Victorian architecture.

Taking the railway West out of London from Paddington, the train passes the factory of Scott's Emulsion, built at Southall in 1906. Scott's Emulsion is a cod-liver oil preparation and on the side of the building facing North on to the railway tracks there is a giant mosaic picture of a fisherman carrying a cod (126, 127). This picture forms a large and permanent advertisement for the firm. Like the Crouch Hill dairy it is particularly happy application of decorative art in a commercial setting. The whole of this face of the building displays an unusual sensitivity with a well-proportioned simplicity in the windows and the placing of the display panel. The first floor is painted in white to

127. Detail of plate 126, Italian mosaic

link the stucco picture surround to the rest of the structure. Above this there is a parapet wall with the name of the company written in white mosaic on a blue ground.

In many of these examples the decoration was also a form of advertising. Because decoration was seen as an integral part of the architecture there was no conflict between the advertisement and the building. This is not the case today. Because decoration has been denied a role in modern architecture advertising has lost the ornamental quality that it once had. As a result it is vulgar in itself and unrelated to its architectural situation. Although the twentieth century has rid itself of many of the worst excesses of Victorian architecture it has also lost many of the best qualities—the proverbial baby has been thrown out with the bath water. The illustrated architecture of the late nineteenth century shows what the Victorians were capable of, at best, and should provide some lessons for contemporary design.

128. Flats in East Finchley, London

7 In Favour of Decoration

Variety, individuality, colour, pattern, curiosity—these are the words
that have been used to describe Victorian architecture. Of course,
architecture of this kind costs money and that is why these qualities,
where they exist in modern architecture, are to be found in buildings
where they can be shown to give a return on investment: in restaurants,
for instance, or boutiques, where the ambience is the thing that draws
the customers.

But even if we accept the reality of economic constraints and the fact
that we cannot afford to do what the Victorians did (even if we had the
men and time to do it!), why is so much building today utilitarian,
crude and aesthetically barren? Is this the necessary consequence of
economy and rationality? During the early decades of the century
there was a freshness and novelty in machine-age architecture and the
ideas generated by the Functional Tradition produced buildings that,
in contrast to the stylistic excesses of the Victorians, were marked by
a simple fitness in design and use of materials. But with the crystallisa-
tion of the International Style modern architecture was to become just
another kind of style, another formula for building, as the Gothic or
Classical styles had been. W. R. Lethaby noted this with disappoint-
ment when he spoke of modern architecture as 'only another kind of

129. High rise flats, East London

130. Mixed development, Bloomsbury, London. The general disposition of the building is quite pleasing when viewed as a whole, from a distance. But the details (131) are often very unsatisfactory: the human scale is subjected to the visual impact of the overall structure. There is a good case here for small decorative detailing to provide visual interest at pedestrian level.

design humbug to pass off with a shrug—ye olde modernist style—we must have a style to copy . . .'* He realised that so much ornament was meaningless, pretentious and moribund and that it had necessarily to be stripped away but fully expected that a new form of decorative expression would take its place. This did not happen. In so many instances under the pretext of being modern and functional architects simply disregarded the visual quality of the building.

Attempts have been made to come to terms with this problem. But because of the universal rejection of applied ornament the archi-

* Lethaby W. R. RIBA *Journal*, 1957, Vol. LXIV; p. 221.

132. St Michael's Primary school—too fickle and
delicate

133. Meaningless and laughable 'modern' decoration

134. An example of a good modern tiled mural

tect has sought to bring visual interest to a building by making the whole structure one big piece of sculpture, exaggerating the form in order to create a dramatic effect. Inventing styles with such picturesque titles as 'bowellism' architects have endeavoured to find a way of making buildings attractive and stimulating. Cleverly cantilevered structures with staircases arcing like flying buttresses testify to the ingenuity of the architect and the technical skill of the engineer. However these things are not only extremely expensive but it is very questionable whether they provide a satisfactory solution to the problem since most people simply would not appreciate such subtleties. We can all perceive the technical genius of the structural engineer when looking at the new Severn Bridge, but it is doubtful whether this is sufficient to involve people in architecture—there is no relationship between viewer and object, nothing to feed the mind or excite the imagination. Buildings that seek novelty and interest by employing complex structural systems do not satisfy the public demand for an

135. A bold attempt at decoration that is reasonably successful, by Pilkington's, Glenrothes, Scotland

136. 'Paradise Bridge', Primrose Hill, North London
137. Detail to plate 136; paintings by Phil Hartigan

architecture that they can understand and relate to. It is very much a case of architects' architecture.

On the rare occasions where an architect has attempted to introduce pictorial decoration (this being the most popular and readily understood form of decoration), however well intentioned the scheme may be, the results are usually pitiful. In schools, for instance, where a blank wall can be used to good effect the designer is often so inhibited that the decoration is quite out of scale, too fickle and delicate (132) or else, afraid to compromise the supposed ideals of modern art, he produces incoherent abstract designs (133). While acknowledging contemporary styles, the conditions for mural decoration are the same today as they were a hundred years ago. The image must be bold, clear and lively with drama and activity. This can still be achieved (134) but we are so out of practice that the most elementary rules of decoration, that were second nature to the youngest student in the nineteenth century, have been forgotten.

No doubt there are those who will remain convinced that ornament and decoration can have no part in modern architecture. But there is no better way of re-establishing the communion between people and architecture. Frank Lloyd Wright said that modern architecture was like a car driving down a *cul de sac* and the truth of this statement is becoming increasingly apparent as the architect tries desperately to devise new forms of expression using reversed ziggurats, cylindrical tower-blocks and other bizarre structures in a way that is more reminiscent of children's building blocks than anything else. There can be no future for architecture when the architect ends up playing with shapes in this way: such irrational formalism fails to achieve either the proper free, creative expression of the Decorative Tradition, or the logic of technological functionalism. The apparent conflict between these two forces which historically have acted in opposite directions, with the added complication that there is now a premium set upon originality, leaves the architect with a seemingly impossible task.

What then can he do about it? Most of the technical aspects of architecture are now controlled by specialists: the structural engineer, the quantity surveyor, servicing, heating, lighting and ventilation consultants. It is fair to suppose that the architect's responsibility now is for the design of the building, that is the allocation of space and the *visual quality* of the structure. If the architect fails to assert the importance of aesthetic values then he is failing in his job. He is then acting not as a citizen but as a slave to technology. It is the architect's task to bridge the gulf between science and humanity within his province which is the built environment. The architect must instil the design with those essential human values of individuality, personality and creativity so that the granting of aesthetic pleasure becomes an essential part of the function of architecture. If he fails in this responsibility then a building is stillborn.

It is, of course, easier to talk of the need to establish such values than to define them. But in our present society there are indications that they are concerned with the need for people to express their own individuality over mass-produced objects and impersonal environ-

138. Carnaby St, London: 'where the music is, there the people dance'

ments. The desire for individuality is recognised well enough by the car and clothing manufacturers who design for personality. We are familiar with the idea of customised cars which are restyled or repainted to provide identity in a uniform object. There are even a few buses in London with multicolour designs which are causing some old ladies to wonder what is happening. But where is the equivalent response from architects?

Something is happening in architecture, in fact, but it is not the work of architects. People have realised that the best way to brighten the streets is to do it themselves and with no more than paint they

139. Street painting of this sort provides colour and
excitement in architecture

140. Oxford St : rainbow coloured chevrons give emphasis and direction

141. A simple and explicit message about architecture

142. Architecture is a political issue—here Victorian buildings in Palace Gate were demolished for redevelopment

are beginning to transform the scene. Street painting is the most promising development in the field of decoration. The railway bridge by Primrose Hill Station in North London (136, 137) is a good example. It used to be painted battleship grey, but now, thanks to the work of Phil Hartigan, it is a blaze of colour. He has also painted a mural above a bookshop in Chalk Farm Road. The paintings may not be to everybody's taste, but there have been few complaints, and plenty of compliments. In an area that could hardly be noted for the quality of its architecture and which is particularly grey and unprepossessing, this bridge has now a gaiety that should encourage similar work. The stylised dragon on a house in Artesian Road, Notting Hill Gate shows a very different approach but it is successful in the same way because it provides interest in an area that is otherwise rather dull. Painting on a house seems a particularly attractive idea and is no more than a logical extension of having pictures inside.

Street painting in Carnaby Street (138, 139) is not so unexpected. People go there for the atmosphere as much as to buy goods and the painted buildings unify the area into a complete experience which is better than the ground level view that shops usually create. Street painting can integrate the building with the activity in one part of it, it can emphasise a certain place or simply focus attention on a local message (141). As well as these rather architectural functions it is a medium for communicating ideas and images in an artistic sense. In Los Angeles, where more street painting has been done than in any other city, there are amazing pieces of work like the Farmer John pig abattoir where the outside walls are covered with ironic pictures of pigs romping in the fields. There are surrealist fantasies, buildings painted with *trompe d'oeil* effects and religious paintings that are a constant witness to the values of the people that live in the area. This is the great thing about street painting. It not only brightens the city but can express the personality of the inhabitants. As things change, so do the paintings—a coat of whitewash and you can start again.

It is valid to make a comparison between street painting and the illustrated architecture of the late nineteenth century. What the Victorians did with tiles, terracotta and mosaic we can now do with paint. Street painting is in the Decorative Tradition and demonstrates some of the possibilities that are available to us. It may be more suited to some areas than others and has particular advantages in brightening old grey buildings. There is no reason, however, why it should not be equally successfully employed on new structures. The arguments in favour of colour and decoration are substantially the same as they were a hundred years ago, but with modern materials we can achieve the same effect with much less difficulty. What we lack is not the technical capacity to produce decorative materials so much as the will to do so.

Street painting is a message from grassroots, where the architect has failed in his responsibility people have supplied the deficiency in the best way that is available. This reassertion of the role of decoration in architecture is clear evidence of the deep-felt need for colour and imagery to brighten the city. One may note the only designed equiva-

143. Sensitive façade painting makes this building a feature

lent in parts of London like Chelsea and Fulham where shops and restaurants have received similar external treatment with painted windows, pictorial signs and period décor. Here a younger generation, untrammelled by the hidebound theories of pre-war thinking, work with an intuitive sureness that is aesthetically pleasing and commercially successful. Finding little outlet for their ideas in architecture as such many of the most able young designers in recent years have moved into interior design and shop-fitting. Here there is an opportunity to design, on a small scale, the sort of architecture that is a clear contemporary expression of the Decorative Tradition.

These small designs and one-off hand-painted murals are not however a satisfactory way of introducing decoration to the whole range of

144. A suitable case for treatment? A North London school

architecture. In large-scale housing schemes or areas of comprehensive redevelopment it is impractical to employ decoration of this sort in any quantity. If decoration is to play any significant part in the future of architecture it will have to be mass-produced, just as it was in the nineteenth century. It has already been suggested that decoration is not inimical to mechanical processes, it only needs the designer to alter the specification for the machine to adapt to the situation, rather than the specification adapting itself to the machine.

It is no use pretending that the re-introduction of decoration will not cost money. The budget rarely allows for more than the direct costs of construction and even if the architect wants to use decoration the client will claim that he cannot afford it. One of the reasons for new buildings being utilitarian, cheap and nasty is the constant pressure of cost which is imposed on the designer. But now that the idea of the 'social responsibility audit' is gaining ground both developer and designer must recognise that the creation of a visually pleasant

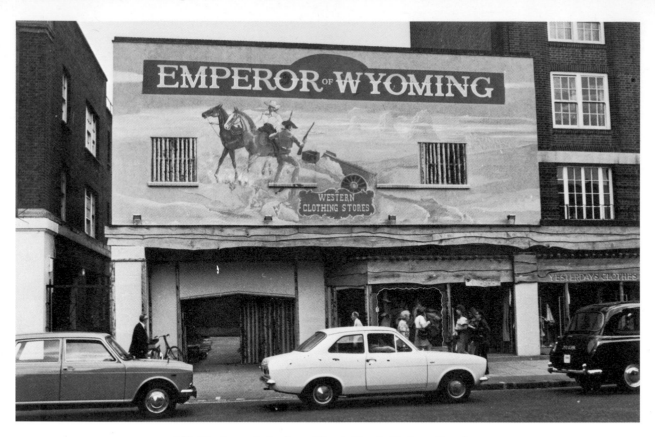

145. Western-style shop, King's Road, Chelsea, London

environment has a social value that has to take precedence over short term economics.

The role of decoration in architecture today may be considered in much the same way as the decoration of the nineteenth century has been examined: under the headings of the function, the potential forms and materials to be used. The prime function of decoration is to enhance the visual quality of a building, Once and for all we should reject the dour puritanism that has gripped architecture for so long and build something that people enjoy. It is unlikely that the present methods of construction will be altered in the foreseeable future and so the visual interest in a building will have to be supplied by applied decoration. The form that this could take will depend on the type of building. In domestic architecture some means should be found of devising less regular and more interesting shapes instead of the rectangular plainness of mock Georgian which has become so universal. In housing estates each unit must differ in some way from its neighbour and so provide individuality. It may well be that this can best be achieved by using small ornamental details in the same way that the Victorians did. If tower blocks have to be built some provision must be made either for a comprehensive scheme of decoration or for the householder to provide some kind of external decoration of his own choosing. Thus decoration can provide identity and individuality and a means of self-expression in an environment that at present is impersonal and anonymous.

In the case of commercial buildings decoration can supply a similar kind of identity, but it is also possible to make use of architectural decoration as a form of advertising. Modern shopping centres show a poverty of imaginative thinking with their bright spotlights on consumer products which make you feel as if you are walking along with blinkers on to prevent you seeing anything but things to buy. But it is possible to use architectural decoration in such a way that it is both an efficient advertisement and a source of visual pleasure and entertainment. This is the way that the Victorians designed and it has its modern equivalent in decorative advertisements like the 'cornucopia' mural on the side of a fruit shop in the Triangle, Clifton, Bristol (148).

One of the factors determining the future of decoration, at least in commercial buildings, is the rapid nature of change of use. This would seem to mean that ornamental forms that permanently describe the function of a building might not be commercially acceptable. Mural painting of the sort that has been described would provide the obvious answer to the problem. In other cases it should be possible to elaborate the house-styling of large chain-stores in such a way that the building provides visual interest as well as a more effective and recognisable form of identity for the group. Again, this was a functional use of decoration that the Victorians employed to good effect. Such advertising is commercially profitable. It is only the restraint imposed by modern theories of design that prevents architects exploiting decoration in this way.

It is out of place here to discuss the morality of advertising, but decoration should also have a non-commercial interest. It should act as a symbolic manifestation of the values of society. In civic buildings, churches or schools decoration should provide a way of expressing not only the purpose of the building and its internal function but should symbolise the traditions, aims and ethics of the community. In schools it can provide a medium for teaching and education, either in the form of professionally designed decoration or as work that the pupils themselves undertake. As Walter Crane observed, architectural decoration should be the highest form of popular art.

The general townscape could be greatly improved by re-introducing decoration into design. Street furniture, signs, pavements and the host of small environmental objects could all be made more interesting, stimulating and ornamental. The plethora of brutal and ugly forms that assault the eye could be made more pleasing and meaningful if more care was taken to use decorative designs with colourful, patterned and textured finishes. One small example will provide sufficient contrast: compare the concrete seats (rarely occupied) in many new town centres with the delightful curving benches that Gaudi designed for Barcelona. Using ornamental shapes and a surface of coloured tiles he provided a simple yet perfect piece of decorative design.

In a general way, decoration can create a more meaningful language of architectural forms. We have become accustomed to the idea that all openings in the structure of a building should be in the same rectangular proportion—the doorway is simply a bigger 'hole' in the grid. The Victorians used various shapes and sizes of ornament, not only to

146. A successful conversion of old premises which echoes the lines of the existing structure

create variety and interest but to produce direction and emphasis within the design. The size and quantity of decorative detailing emphasised the important parts of the building; it was impossible to mistake the doorway, for instance, since this was the climax of the façade design. In the same way the name of the building and, interpreted through decorative images, its function were given clear prominence in the design. Floor levels, circulation patterns, the different rooms and their various functions, every aspect of the design right down to the chimney stacks was clearly articulated and could be 'read' with little difficulty from the outside of the building. It is important to be able to do this since it allows one to understand a building and its

147. By contrast, little attempt appears to have been made here to blend old and new structures, with appalling results

structure and ways of operating. This is particularly significant when one considers the way that children relate to architecture. They navigate entirely by means of images and in these high-rise blocks of flats they often get lost because there is no meaningful language of architectural symbols. The anonymous façades of modern architecture make no provision for understanding and rely instead on notices saying 'main entrance' and a complex numbering system that often only adds to the confusion.

The exact form that modern architectural decoration will take is uncertain. There is a full range of possibilities including the use of

148. Painted advertisement, The Triangle, Bristol

colour, texture, pattern, ornamental forms and images. The nineteenth-century designers made use of all of these, especially pictorial
and sculptural images; where decoration has been used in modern
architecture it has rarely developed beyond texture and occasionally
pattern or colour. The Victorians made particular use of naturalistic
decoration and we might do worse than follow this example. But contemporary society is so at odds with itself that it is not easy to say what
is a universally acceptable iconography today (pictures of grinning
astronauts would hardly be suitable). The sort of geometric patterns
that are sometimes used (149) show how inhibited designers are, using
awkward shapes and clumsy patterns with no freedom or movement.
If the designer was once able to liberate himself from this gawky
angularity it is likely that new and attractive forms would emerge.
In view of the recent revival of interest in Victorian design it seems
possible that we may, in the first instance, use some of the nineteenth-
century decorative styles and that from this imitation more original
ideas may develop.

It is arguable that the flowering of the Decorative Tradition in the
late nineteenth century was closely linked to the establishment of
government schools of art and design in the middle decades of the
century. Any real resurgence of ornamental art at this time must be
the result of a similar impetus. There is a need for an integrated schooling based on the role of the decorative arts in architecture. During the
last ten years there has been a renaissance in the field of graphics,
largely as a result of changes in art school training and a similar move-

149. Modern concrete finishes on tower blocks, Victoria, London

ment is needed to build a firm foundation for architectural decoration. The subject is not considered at all in architectural education at the present time. If courses were set up in art schools and colleges there can be no doubt that fresh thinking would quickly emerge and from thence would be born the ornamental forms that are suitable to contemporary society.

The evolution of modern decorative forms is clearly related to materials although materials, in themselves, cannot provide a solution to the problem of what these forms should be. A great deal is made of the importance of materials in modern architecture—materials that weather in a particular way, that are easy to handle and adaptable to prefabrication and so on. But even if no effort was made in other directions the quality of these materials could be greatly improved. Not the performance standard but the aesthetic quality. Concrete, which is now used as universally as terracotta was in the nineteenth century, is capable of much more imaginative treatment. Somebody once had the idea of giving concrete a surface patina by accentuating the imprint of the shuttering boards. That was an idea, one idea and not very special at that. Concrete aggregates have been used which, when they are sand-blasted, reveal the surface texture and some small colour contrast, though they never achieve any real liveliness. Is it really the best that can be done with concrete? Why can it not be brightly coloured with permanent dyes ('think of whole buildings vibrating with harmonies of colour'), why is it not cast into something

139

resembling an attractive form instead of all those ugly angular shapes? Other materials could be used to provide a bright and colourful surface texture: colour glass would catch the light and reflect colours on to the street and if it was sand-blasted it would have that lovely texture of glass pebbles found on the sea-shore. Broken tile with brightly coloured glazes could easily be cast into prefabricated panels, with colour contrast and unit size responding to the location of the panel on the elevation. Perhaps it would even be possible to have some proper mosaics at street level where they can be seen by pedestrians.

It may be possible to improve concrete and make it more attractive and less mechanical and inhuman. But failing that it is imperative that we employ other materials. Brick is still the most traditional building fabric in England and capable of receiving surface treatment (as in the nineteenth century) and permanent colouring. By combining different coloured bricks it is possible to achieve striking effects, as Butterfield's 'constructional polychromy' showed a hundred years ago. If it is impossible to devise new ideas there are precedents like this to follow. New materials will also evolve, though it is the architects' responsibility to ask for them and to provide the specification. Synthetic fabrics have not been fully developed as yet and may well provide the answer to present demands. Alternatively a modern terracotta may be developed at a reasonable cost that would compete with precast concrete and provide endless possibilities for decoration.

Other traditional materials could also be used if the manufacturers reconsidered their approach to design. Ceramic tiles still provide one of the best mediums for mural decoration as the new underground stations on the Victoria line demonstrate, though the designs are singularly uninspired. Whether the tiles are screen printed or hand painted it is possible to develop more attractive images and a wider, more imaginative range of designs that could be made available to the popular market. Tiles could be used in exactly the same way as in the nineteenth century as panels in porches and as murals in other sheltered positions. Geometric pavements could be re-introduced along with pictorial floor mosaics (a traditional form of decoration if ever there was one) and modern screen-printed floor tiles. Coloured glass is still available, it only needs the architect to specify its use. The creative use of metal is totally neglected in modern architecture and it is sad to see such a delicate material so completely abused. Balconies, iron railings, metal staircases and gates, all are used still in architecture but as always the design has been stultified by the supposition that to be absolutely modern there must be no pattern or surface decoration other than that provided by the bare structural outlines of the object— a fence is simply a row of rods, a balcony rail a scaffolding tube set into concrete posts. There is plenty of scope here for decoration.

Whatever materials are used in modern architectural decoration they will have to be manufactured cheaply. In the context of factory production this usually implies a limited number of designs and the consequent limitation of the stock list. It is important that this should not be the case here since it is imperative that there should be the widest possible choice. Variety is an essential ingredient of decorative architecture, whether the ornamental elements are selected by the architect or an individual. It will take time for mass-produced decoration to become generally available since, of economic necessity, the demand must first be generated. As usual in these cases it is a matter of the chicken and the egg.

But we may be sure that this demand will be generated. There is a growing awareness among people of the importance of architecture and a critical reaction against the aesthetic poverty of contemporary design. Undoubtedly there is a need for inspiration and the development of a colourful, imaginative form of architecture with an iconography that can express something of the delight we feel in living. What this contemporary iconography is we cannot say. This book was compiled in the belief that it must be found and that it will be associated with decoration and the opportunity that decoration provides for personalising the environment. When it is found and expressed in architectural terms we shall know—it will be apparent in the public response when people once again *want to look at and experience architecture*.

150. What Next? Street painting may provide the best form of modern mural decoration: it is colourful, easily applied and quickly altered to suit the changing function of the building

Bibliography

The following list is a select one

Arts and Crafts Society, *Art & Life in the Building and Decoration of Cities*; 1896.

Banham, Reyner, *Theory and Design in the First Machine Age*; 1960.

Clark, Sir Kenneth, *The Gothic Revival*; 1928.

Crosby, Theo, *The Necessary Monument*; 1970.

Eastlake, Charles, *A History of the Gothic Revival*; 1872.

Ferriday, Peter (Ed), *Victorian Architecture*; 1963.

Gloag, John, *Victorian Taste*; 1962.

Hitchcock, H. R. *Architecture of the Nineteenth and Twentieth Centuries*; 1958.

Hussey, Christopher, *The Picturesque*; 1927.

Macleod, Robert, *Style and Society*; 1971.

National Association for the Advancement of Art and Its Application to Industry, proceedings; 1888.

Pevsner, Sir Nikolaus, *The Sources of Modern Architecture and Design*; 1968.

    and Sir J. M. Richards, *The Anti-Rationalists*; 1973.

Rendel, Goodhart, *English Architecture since Regency*; 1953.

Richards, Sir J. M. *The Functional Tradition in early Industrial Buildings*; 1958.

    Introduction to Modern Architecture; 1940.

Ruskin, Sir John, *Complete Works*; 1903.

Summerson, Sir John, *Heavenly Mansions & Other Essays*; 1949.

    Victorian Architecture; 1970.

Townsend, C. H. *Mosaic & Fresco*; 1894.

Venturi, Robert, *Learning from Las Vegas*; 1972.

Index

143